The Talisman Magick
WORKBOOK

Master Your Destiny Through the Use of Talismans

By Kala and Ketz Pajeon

". . . when art is properly understood we will
be able to paint pictures to cure toothaches."
— Pablo Picasso, 1881–1973
Spanish Painter and Sculptor

A Citadel Press Book
Published by Carol Publishing Group

To the Goddess Arynna, who promised
to aid all who called; and to Sophia, the
Goddess of Wisdom, for opening my eyes.

A Citadel Press Book
Published by Carol Publishing Group
Citadel Press is a registered trademark of Carol Communications, Inc.

Editorial Offices: 600 Madison Avenue, New York, N.Y. 10022
Sales & Distribution Offices: 120 Enterprise Avenue, Secaucus, N.J. 07094
In Canada: Canadian Manda Group, P.O. Box 920, Station U,
    Toronto, Ontario M8Z 5P9

Queries regarding rights and permissions should be addressed to Carol
Publishing Group, 600 Madison Avenue, New York, N.Y. 10022

Carol Publishing Group books are available at special discounts for bulk
purchases, for sales promotions, fund raising, or educational purposes.
Special editions can be created to specifications. For details contact:
Special Sales Department, Carol Publishing Group, 120 Enterprise Avenue,
Secaucus, N.J. 07094

Manufactured in the United States of America
10 9 8 7 6 5 4 3 2 1

Library of Congress Cataloging-in-Publicaton Data

Pajeon, Kala.
    The talismatic magick workbook : master your destiny through the use
of talismans / by Kala and Katz Pajeon.
    p. cm.
    "A Citadel Press book."
    ISBN 0-8065-1366-7 (pbk.)
    1. Talismans. I. Pajeon, Katz. II. Title.
BF1561.P35   1992
133.4'4—dc20   92-28896
                                                        CIP

Contents

PART SIX
APPENDICES

List of Tables

Foreword

The Talisman Magick Workbook is one of the best self-help books we have had the privilege of reviewing in recent years. All too often books of this type do not get down to helping people in real situations; but this one cuts through all the cape-swishing and quickly gets down to real work—work that can help you in every phase of daily life. The book presents a good range of approaches with many options that you can tune into from your own ethnic background. By selecting your option, you can be surer that the results will fit your circumstances.

The *Workbook* covers a wide range of different situations where magick can be of help in daily life. Many of the situations you might not have thought of as being amenable to a magickal approach; but the authors show how magickal techniques can help you. They display a thoroughgoing knowledge of many traditional occult disciplines and, with a candor rarely expressed nowadays, show how these traditional methods can be adapted to your problems.

If you know absolutely nothing of the occult or magickal procedures, this book will still help you, for the methods are thoroughly explained and easy, step-by-step instructions are given. If you are skilled in occult matters, the book will help you as well, for it gives an excellent summary of the work and very thoroughly correlates the deities of many cultures to the zodiac and to intent.

In all, we have high praise for the *Workbook*. It belongs in the library both of advanced workers and of neophytes. We look forward to seeing many more works from these capable and experienced writers.

—Gavin and Yvonne Frost
School of Wicca
P.O. Box 1502
New Bern, NC 28563

Preface

As authors of various books and articles concerning the realm of magick, Kala and I often receive letters offering both praise and criticism. We welcome such input from our readers and fellow authors. It is from this type of correspondence that we learn what is sought after by the readers of magickal texts and what is not. We then incorporate these desires into our future works.

The letters from fellow authors normally offer advice and constructive criticism that are greatly appreciated. There are, at times, letters that place judgments on our works which tell us that the writers have entirely misunderstood our intent in presenting a topic in a specific manner.

A case in point was a letter Kala received from a dear friend, whom we had asked to review specific parts of *The Talisman Magick Workbook*.

The writer stated that there is a basic assumption in this book that it is okay to dissipate or destroy someone else or their well being! Or drain away the energy of another, or to coerce others.

The writer further stated that our information, if not our commentaries, definitely suggested these uses, whether we recommended them or not! The writer also feared that a young reader, who felt desperate or was angry with someone, was given that possibility, many times over, in our suggested uses of Cards, Runes and I Ching symbols.

Kala and I feel that the writer is entirely correct, but only to a point. We feel that hiding behind a guise of pretending there is no way that magickal knowledge should be dispensed other than in a positive, i.e, "White Magick," style is as wrong as keeping safe sex information out of the hands of teenagers.

We both feel that ignorance of the full uses to which a talismanic symbol might be put could do more harm than giving the reader the choice of incurring karmic repercussions by the "improper" use of magick.

Ignorance is *not* bliss. Ignorance is dangerous and only a fully informed person can properly decide which path to follow.

Imagine the karmic harm that might be wrought upon a well meaning magickan who ignorantly uses the reverse position of a card, a Rune symbol on a waning rather than a waxing moon, or an I Ching hexagram in the wrong zodiac house. Good intentions do not count in the dispensing of universal lessons. Only by an intelligent understanding of *all* the uses of a talismanic symbol can such incidents be avoided.

There are times when to "dissipate and destroy" are entirely correct uses for talismanic symbols. The destruction of disease and jealousy are but two. "Draining the energy of another" who is bent on destroying himself gives that person time to reconsider his actions. In other words, Yes, there are aspects of all talismanic symbols that can be used to harm other individuals; but is ignorance or the withholding of this information the answer?

As an analogy, place yourself in the role of a parent. You realize that it is impossible to protect your child from life's problems because he or she is not always in your presence. They attend school, go to playgrounds, beaches and parks. They incur the usual skinned knees, occasional fights with the local bully and, generally view life first hand. You cannot constantly be present during the growing years of your child, so how can you, as a well intentioned parent, protect them from afar? You educate them.

As a loving parent, you offer advice on how to react to the realities of life. You attempt to instill into them your own views on morality; arm them with the truth about drugs, fast cars, and sex, all the time knowing that they are going to experiment with life and test your teachings at every opportunity.

Like the young child instructed by loving parents, the novice magickan must be instructed in the morals, ethics and fundamentals of magick. He or she must then experiment and test those teachings so as to form a personal mode of conduct.

It is our philosophy to teach what we know. We take every opportunity to expound on our moral and ethical views when appropriate but we do not believe in holding back knowledge that others might misuse.

As the child learns about the realities of life and suffers the skinned knees and hurt feelings, so the novice magickan will suffer karmic skinned knees and an occasional karmic black eye. This is normal in both the physical and magickal growth processes.

What sets the responsible student of magick apart is the knowledge of right and wrong received through the crown chakra. This is also where the energy for magick is received. If the crown chakra is blocked, as is the case with most amoral people, magick cannot be properly performed and will never leave the sender.

For those students who work around and through temptations for mischief, more power is given. They grow into powerful and moral magickans. Others that fall prey to their own frailties seldom, if ever, achieve enough power to perform true magick.

There are people in this world who will harm others no matter how many attempts are made to conceal information from them. There are far more, in our opinion, who will be unjustly harmed if that information is withheld and they act out of ignorance. It is with that thought in mind that our texts reveal all aspects of the magickal topic under discussion at the time.

We have created *The Talisman Magick Workbook* to properly inform those well meaning readers out there in the real world of the full magickal applications to which each talismanic symbol might be put. By doing so, we hope that anyone reading this work will not inadvertently fall prey to karmic repercussions through ignorant behavior. Should the symbols be employed with the intent to harm another unjustly, then that magickan will be doing so with the full knowledge of the consequences. We have given a view that is not presented through rose colored glasses but one that totally informs people of the full meaning of magick. How that information is used is entirely up to the individual. For far too long, in our opinion, some well intentioned and some not so well intentioned people have felt that to keep someone in ignorance was a way of protecting or controlling them. We totally disagree with that philosophy. It is only through the dispensing of the full truth that intelligent people can make intelligent decisions.

Our largest group of supporters have, interestingly enough, been the informed solitary practitioners, new readers, and experienced students of the occult. We have received numerous letters thanking us for our honest portrayal of magick and the frank way we speak of ethics. They felt we were giving them the tools to make responsible choices based on free will.

The attitude that expresses the philosophy that "I am my brother's or sister's keeper" and "I know what is best for them because I know more" is as outdated as the Inquisition. Kala and I firmly believe that to deny anyone their right to exercise free will and free choice is the worst form of "Black Magick." The pagan who expounds protectionism through ignorance is merely aping the fundamentalist Christian doctrine of subordination.

—KETZ PAJEON, 1992

Acknowledgments

We gratefully appreciate the kind assistance we have received from the following people: Ms. Betty Baxter, who teaches the Carl Payne Toby method of Astrology, a course we highly recommend; and Ms. Louise Huebner, an inspiration to Kala since Kala was sixteen years old.

PART ONE

Introduction

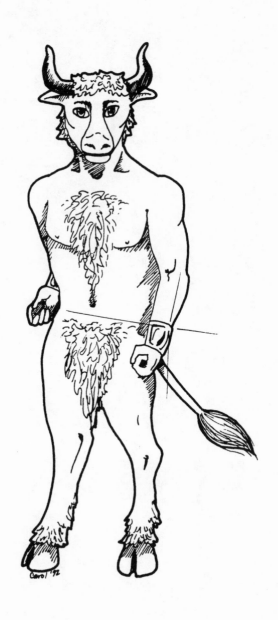

1

What the Reader Can Expect to Learn

Once you have completed this text, you will understand how and why talisman magick really works; knowledge rarely found in books of this type, as it is a well kept secret by most adepts. You will come to understand that all matter is composed of energy. Each particle of matter, from the smallest individual atom to the most complex organism, vibrates to a frequency unique unto itself. By taking advantage of this uniqueness, you can construct talismans of the exact material(s) most conducive to the proper performance for which the talismans are designed.

You will be able to use this knowledge to confidently create a variety of very effective talismans that incorporate both ancient and modern symbols. You will also learn to differentiate between a real talisman and a fake talisman. One that might look very mysterious, but would not hold to the vibrational patterns necessary to perform the correct magickal function. Unless the shapes and symbols making up a talisman are correct, the talisman may be worthless or, worse yet, dangerous to the owner.

Imagine looking into an old grimoire and being able to tell if the talismans presented in the text will in fact work.

Further, you will learn that there are only a few rudimentary lines that make up a vast majority of symbols. For that reason, you will acquire skill in deciphering the meaning of otherwise clandestine symbols. You will learn to alter, repair, and even improve on some original talismans.

Finally, you will be shown how many of the old and mysterious powers, and secrets of talisman construction, can be found in a modern deck of Playing Cards or Tarot Cards, or in the symbology of the I Ching and Runes.

It is unnecessary to create complicated talismans from scratch, unless that is your personal preference. Instead, the same or better effects and results are available by combining the wide variety of popular methods of divination with the Zodiac Worksheet.

There are distinct advantages to using ordinary methods of divination as talismans, the main one being that almost everyone is familiar with them.

Anyone who has ever studied these concepts is well aware of the innate power hidden within each symbol. However, few know how to use them as potent talismans. You will learn that secret from this workbook. Few books go into such detail and depth as this one, and fewer still take the time to analyze what intricate and magickal components are required to create a real, working talisman. It is with this thought in mind that *The Talisman Magick Workbook* was created. Welcome to real talisman magick.

QUICK, EASY TALISMANS USING THE ZODIAC WORKSHEET

As an example of how this book differs from the normal text on talisman magick, refer to the Zodiac Worksheet found at the end of the book. This worksheet will serve as the basis for construction of a useful and potent talisman that differs from the norm only in its simplicity. The method demonstrated here will prove that talisman construction need not be complicated and cloaked in mystery, can be quite simple and fast, but still unbelievably potent in its effect.

As you will soon discover, several chapters in this book are dedicated to an overview of I Ching, Runes, Tarot and ordinary Playing Cards. The reason for including the chapters on divination subjects is that each of these contain intricate symbols that can be used in talisman construction. Here are some examples of how several of our students have successfully used the information provided in this workbook:

ANNA

Anna is a young woman working in the Silicon Valley of California. Until very recently, her social life was in shambles and no one seemed to notice the extreme effort she was putting into her assignments at work. She decided to change all that after taking a class in Talisman Magick.

Not wanting to involve herself in the time-consuming task of memorizing complicated symbols for her talisman, Anna opted for an ordinary deck of playing cards. Using the Fifth House (Leo) for matters of the heart, she placed two Pages (one of Hearts and one of Clubs to stimulate her social life) and two Aces (one of Diamonds and one of Hearts for new beginnings in money and love) within this house on her Zodiac Worksheet. For popularity, she also placed three nines (one each of Hearts, Clubs, and Diamonds) in the Eleventh House (Aquarius). To influence her boss at work, she placed three Kings (one each of Spades, Diamonds, and Clubs) in the Tenth House (Capricorn). She reported that soon after completing and energizing her talisman, she began a busy dating schedule with a rich executive and is due for a promotion at work.

ROBERT

Robert is a college student who likes to use the alpha and numerical symbols in various zodiac houses to achieve his desires. He especially uses them to enhance his memory and comprehension when studying for exams. His favorite houses are the Third House (Gemini), for his memory, and the Ninth House (Sagittarius) for recognition of his work.

Robert places the grade he wants to achieve, along with the name of his instructor, in the proper houses and has yet to fail a course.

TINA

Tina is a fifth generation Chinese American. Her ancestors migrated to the United States in the 1800s. The family was hard working and progressive. They insisted that all of the children

Zodiac Worksheet

ANNA WILLIAMS

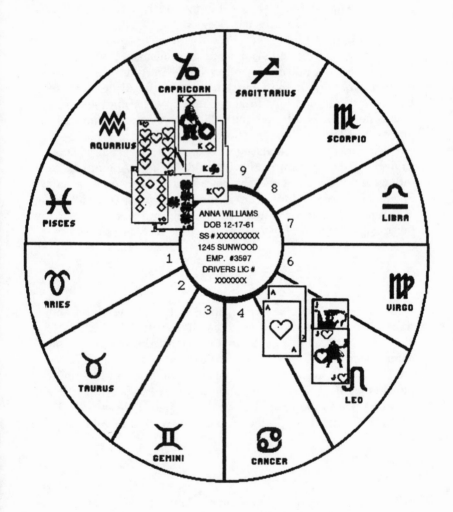

Zodiac Worksheet

ROBERT ATKINS

Zodiac wheel with twelve signs:

CAPRICORN ♑ — MR. HILL'S POLITICAL SCIENCE CLASS 103 GRADE= A

SAGITTARIUS ♐ — JOHNSON'S TEXT OF POLITICAL SCIENCE

SCORPIO ♏

AQUARIUS ♒

LIBRA ♎

PISCES ♓

ARIES ♈

VIRGO ♍

TAURUS ♉

LEO ♌

GEMINI ♊

CANCER ♋

IINCREASE MEMORY POWER

Center:
ROB ATKINS
DOB 5-12-65
78 HAWK ST.
STUDENT #
11345-B
SS # XXXXXX
DRIVER LIC.
XXXXXXXXX

Numbers around inner circle: 10, 9, 8, 11, 12, 7, 1, 6, 2, 5, 3, 4 become thoroughly educated and indoctrinated into the western way of life while still maintaining their cultural roots.

Combining the knowledge of the I Ching, which she had acquired through her heritage, and the knowledge of Astrology she had acquired in our workshops, she created a distinctive and integrated Zodiac Worksheet.

Tina replaced all the symbols on the "western" Zodiac Worksheet with more traditional Chinese characters. The result was esthetically beautiful and magickally effective as shown in the following diagram.

Tina stated that she had found no difficulty in using the Chinese I Ching symbols when creating her talisman, after she realized just what a talisman actually was. It has protected her apartment and possessions from theft and vandalism for nearly three years while friends and neighbors have suffered such violations in the same complex. Here is what she did:

Tina chose three zodiac houses in which to place her I Ching symbols and assembled her talisman on a waxing moon.

In the Twelfth House (Pisces), Hidden Enemies, Losses, and Theft, she placed #40, Hsieh, Deliverance, and #56, Lu, The Wanderer (representing the thief).

In the Fourth House (Cancer), which represented her home itself, she placed #1, Ch'ien, Strong Creative Power (this increased her abilities to protect her home with magick); #14, Ta Yu, Possessions in Great Measure (representing all within her home), and #60, Chieh, Limit (blocking the thief from entering the home).

Lastly, she placed in the Seventh House (Libra), under Open Enemies, #59, Haun, Dispersion (representing her enemies fleeing from her).

Tina stated that on the waxing moon, for approximately two weeks, she would bring out her talisman and burn one blue candle within its center. So far, no one has ever robbed her home.

RON AND ROCHELLE

Ron and Rochelle, after four years of marriage and two adorable children, are still very much in love.

Zodiac Worksheet
Tina Chu

TINA CHU
DOB 7-25-51.
768 HILL ST.
SAN FRANCISCO
CALIF. XXXXX
TELEPHONE XXXX
APARTMENT 4

ROOSTER

MONKEY

GOAT

DOG

PIG   40   56

HORSE   59

MOUSE

SNAKE

BULL

DRAGON

CAT

RABBIT

10 9 8 11 12 1 2 3 4 5 6 7

1 14 6

WESTERN EQUIVALENT CHART
1—ARIES
2—TAURUS
3—GEMINI
4—CANCER

5—LEO
6—VIRGO
7—LIBRA

8—SCORPIO
9—SAGITTARIUS
10—CAPRICORN
11—AQUARIUS
12—PISCES

To protect their special love relationship, children, and home, Ron placed #24 Othalaz, the rune of possession and protection, and, #8 Wunjo, the rune of success and happiness, within the zodiac house of Cancer.

This combination assures a happy and successful marriage, home life, and family relationship. It provides protection for everyone living within the home.

To provide for his family, Ron placed #1 Fehu, the rune of speedy money and abundance, into the zodiac house of Taurus (wealth). And, since Rochelle works very hard as a freelance photographer, he also placed #12 Jera, the rune of reaping profits of work and labor, into Taurus. The combination of Fehu and Jera insures that Rochelle will be paid quickly for the work she does.

Finally, Rochelle placed two runes within Leo, #18 Beorc, and #6, Kaunaz. Beorc was used to ensure peace and harmony among their existing two children, as she and Ron were planning for a third child. She also knew that Beorc would help assure that she was a good mother and would not let her career overshadow her obligations as a parent.

Kaunaz was included in Leo so that her children would add to her creative abilities rather than distract from them. Rochelle wanted to enjoy her role as a mother as well as her photography career.

KALA
(A personal experience)

I have found that no matter what I want to use as a symbol in my Talisman Magick, my subconscious is always two steps ahead of me. I have used the Runes, Playing Cards, the Tarot, and the I Ching, along with a variety of homemade characters with excellent results.

For that reason, I personally do not believe one method to be superior to another. On the contrary, from the reports of my students and from my personal experience, I believe it is best to use whatever feels comfortable and, therefore, I gravitate toward Playing Cards or the Tarot.

As for the effectiveness of the Zodiac Worksheet method of Talisman Magick in my own life, I have the perfect example for

Zodiac Worksheet
RONALD AND ROCHELLE REMINGTON

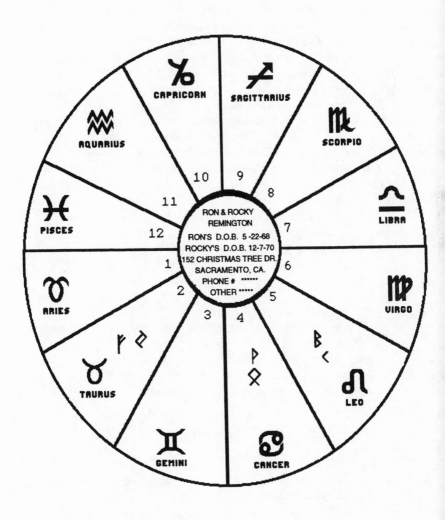

you. I had written two short stories and submitted them to three magazines. Being very busy, as my life always seems to be, I put the stories out of my mind as soon as they were submitted. They were suddenly very real again when I received two rejection notices back to back.

From my worn deck of Tarot cards, I selected the High Priestess, the Sun, the Three of Pentacles, and the Ace of Pentacles. I placed the first three cards within the Ninth House (Sagittarius), knowing that it rules publishing. The last card, the Ace of Pentacles, I placed in the Sixth House (Virgo), knowing that it rules services performed for a fee. Most certainly I wanted to get paid for my work as well as being published.

It took exactly twenty-four hours before I received my response by telephone. I had sold both my stories to the last magazine and the publisher wanted to see a third. I was ecstatic.

In closing here, I just want to pass on one more thing. Many of my students have told me that the more they use the Zodiac Worksheet system of Talisman Magick, the stronger it seems to be and the faster it works. I can't deny that. Twenty-four hours was quick enough for me.

Chapter 1 Quiz

1. All matter is composed of energy. T-F
2. An incorrectly made talisman is of no consequence as it won't work anyway. T-F
3. Playing cards are of no use as talismans. T-F
4. Anna chose Leo to enhance her social life. T-F
5. Robert chose Gemini to gain recognition. T-F

Answers

1. True.
2. False. It may be quite dangerous as even an incorrectly made talisman will work, however inefficiently.
3. False. They are potent talismans as well as divination devices.
4. True.
5. False. He chose it to enhance his memory.

2

About Talismans

WHAT IS A TALISMAN?

Almost any object you might envision has the potential for becoming a talisman. Perhaps you have seen people who possess a "lucky 4-leaf clover" or a "lucky rabbit's foot" or wear a medallion or cross about their neck. How about the plastic religious icon on the dashboard of a car or truck? These are all forms of talismans, though normally they are relegated to the "lucky charm" or "devotional" categories.

What differentiates mere "lucky" or "devotional" pieces from real magickal talismans? Basically, there are three important criteria that a talisman must meet to be termed "real." 1: A real talisman must be programmed by energizing techniques similar to those discussed later in this text. 2: The shapes, the construction materials, and the geometric designs adorning the talisman must conform to magickal rules, guidelines or practices. 3: The creation of the talisman must be in conformance with the proper universal or astrological planetary alignment.

WHY ARE TALISMANS CREATED?

A talisman is created in order to bring about a change in accordance with the will of the creator. As an example, let us suppose you want to become lucky in gambling. With this "change" in mind, a talisman is constructed to manifest this desire. The same would hold true for whatever purpose or "change" is desired, be it to obtain love, money, protection, or health, or the elimination of disease, bad habits, or negative influences.

DO I NEED ANY SPECIAL SKILLS OR KNOWLEDGE?

Everything that you need to know in order to create a talisman is provided within this text. Some knowledge of magick and astrology is helpful but not necessary. We will progress from the very basic and rudimentary talismans and finally end up with some surprising variations using everything from ordinary playing and tarot cards to the symbols of Runes and the I Ching.

HOW DOES A TALISMAN WORK?

Any object or symbol, used for one specific purpose, for a very long period of time, soon becomes a reservoir of energy and thus a source of power for those who know how to tap into it. This is true because every time someone thinks (which is directed energy) about an object or symbol, they are enhancing it with customized energy. This energy is molded by the sender's emotions and thoughts. The energy embodied within can be either of a constructive or destructive nature.

Consider now the millions of minds over thousands of years that have sincerely believed that a mythological being actually existed, or that a certain object, symbol, or word possessed the power to manifest the desire or will of the believer. Those very beings have assumed a "life force" and the objects, symbols, and words have taken on and stored the potent energy put forth by those minds.

By creating a magickal representation of those objects, symbols, words, or beings, of the proper materials and at the proper time, we can create an object capable of influencing the universal energies around us. Thus we have a talisman, an object by which the universal forces are directed to manifest our goals and desires.

WHO USES TALISMANS?

Anyone can learn to use a talisman. Those that apply themselves and master how to actually tap into this age-old source of energy will find unlimited power at their disposal. Others who do not know the full secrets of the talisman's magickal properties and/or do not know how to correctly harness the potent energy sources, create nothing but the mere "lucky" pieces that adorn the many gift shops.

HOW DO I TAP INTO THIS ENERGY?

Before we discuss the energizing of a talisman and why it reacts to your mental output by way of creative visualization, let's talk about how those energies are created in the first place.

As stated earlier, millions of minds thinking the same thoughts over thousands of years create enormous stores of energy. This energy "creates" that which was previously "uncreated." As an example, mythical beings, animals, and concepts all start out as mere ideas in dreams or daydreams. The more they are thought of, the more "real" they become. Thus, their ability to influence by independent function and manifestation grows in direct proportion. They become as myths to a large segment of the population and thus influence that population's actions and beliefs. (The term myth here is used as the modern philosophers use the term paradigm: a pattern, example, or model.)

So, what does this mean to you when creating a talisman? It means that any concepts, beings, or symbols, whether in the forms of Gods, Goddesses, Saints, Loas, Spirits, Demons, Devils, Angels, or geometric shapes, become, after a long period of energy absorption and use, independent functioning centers of pure energy and power and, in some cases, living entities.

This is why many of the medieval magickans called upon certain Angels, Demons, or Demi-Gods to empower, energize, and activate their talismans. In fact, by doing so, the talisman never lost power, as it was continually drawing from its unlimited source, the energy generated by millions of minds.

There is one problem, though, when tapping into power such as this. When the object or deity becomes unpopular or another takes its place, the power source begins to wane. As time passes and the source of power diminishes in size and strength—i.e. people begin to disbelieve in the particular object or deity—the object's usefulness and reliability pass into obscurity, or the deity fades into non-existence. When people say that a god is dead or a concept dies, that is very true. The power that manifested it ceased to be, therefore it also ceased to be.

With this understanding in mind, it is very important for you to realize that if you believe that there is goodness or wickedness lurking somewhere out there in the universe just waiting for you to tap into its power, you will surely find it. *To believe something exists is the first step in making it so.* Conversely, *the first step in destroying something is to deny it the energy of belief.* This concept underlies the basis for most Pagan thinking. Pagans do not acknowledge "evil" as a fact but as a concept created in the minds of those who wish to dominate and enslave those whose religious and political beliefs conflict with theirs. Most pagans, by refusing to acknowledge that "evil" exists, deny those who would harm others the power source of energy they need to survive. This action inhibits the "evil" human mind. The true pagan does not see or experience the world as say a Christian would. Those sects that believe in evil demons and devils, and the concept that evil lurks behind every corner just waiting to tempt them into misconduct, will indeed find their beliefs to be true. They made them, they feed them, so they must live with them.

Many of the ancient talismans and talismanic symbols, especially those of a religious nature, still retain potent power as they are still thought of on a daily basis. Many were created with evil intent and bear the names of devils, demons, and fallen angels. No one should attempt to make an ancient talisman without first having become familiarized with the philosophy behind the symbol(s).

Now, let us move on to the tapping of the power source in order to energize a talisman.

After the physical creation of the talisman, learned later in this text, the next step will be to either imbue it with your own energy or to tap into a source of energy that will enhance the latent power of the material making up the talisman.

As explained earlier, the human mind possesses great power in the form of electrical energy. By channeling that energy into the talisman, you activate its power or enhance its latent power to manifest the desire or goal for which it was created. The material from which the talisman is constructed, along with the symbols upon it, vibrate at certain frequencies of energy. By visualizing that energy and mentally concentrating it into the talisman, you create a powerful tool. The properly constructed and energized talisman, either singularly or in a combination of acts, literally attracts, repels, absorbs, expels, manifests, or destroys that goal or desire of the magickan.

This energizing technique, which employs the power of the mind, is called Creative Visualization. Creative Visualization is not difficult. As an example, how about the time you desperately wanted a change in your life, or your health, so you clasped a coin in your hand, wished with all your heart, and then threw that coin into a fountain? Maybe you have carved initials on a tree while dreaming of true love? If you have, you have taken the first steps toward creatively visualizing your desire, just as you would when energizing a talisman. In fact, the coin and the tree became talismans of a sort. They both received your mental energy and were transformed into talismans by the power of your mind. The symbols on the coin and the construction of the coin may not have aided your desires, but they, in a very minor way, worked for you. The symbols placed on the tree were also additive to the mental power you put forth and thus the tree became a more powerful talisman than one without any symbols placed upon it.

Creative Visualization is a form of controlled self-hypnosis or daydreaming. You create an object, desire, or situation in your mind and thus make it real. The more you concentrate, the more real it becomes. With practice, you will find that you are able to see, clearly within your own mind, that which you desire most.

Chapter 2 Quiz

1. A "real talisman" must be energized. T-F
2. Why did many of the medieval magickans call upon certain Angels, Demons, or Demi-Gods to empower their talismans?
3. To believe that something exists does not make it real. T-F
4. If you have ever made a wish and thrown a coin into a fountain, you have created a form of talisman. T-F
5. Creative Visualization has nothing to do with self-hypnosis or daydreaming. T-F

Answers

1. True.
2. They represented an unlimited source of power that had been generated by millions of minds.
3. False. Believing is the first step of manifestation.
4. True.
5. False. Creative Visualization is a form of them both.

PART TWO

The Zodiac
The Key to Quick and Easy Talismans

3

An Introduction to Astrology

At the exact moment in time that you were born, the universe, in the uniqueness of the moment, manifested your goals, your lessons, and your potentialities. You chose to be born at the exact moment in time that would provide the correct alignment of the universe deemed necessary for the achievements of this incarnation.

For some individuals, this present incarnation may be rife with lessons that make life seem extremely difficult and unpleasant. While for others, the fortunate few, the lessons may be simple and easy to understand, resulting in a very pleasant existence.

Should you be one of those individuals whose life seems forever blocked by difficulties, the knowledge of astrology and its application to talisman magick will help you to control and manipulate these influences and, in general, increase your enjoyment of life.

Talismans, created and used under the correct astrological influences, are some of the most powerful tools available to the magickan. As the science of astrology provides clues to the universe's influences over every aspect of life, your goal is to control and manipulate these influences that were programmed at the moment of your birth.

By exercising this control, you create your own destiny while still fulfilling your goals and learning any lessons necessary for progression.

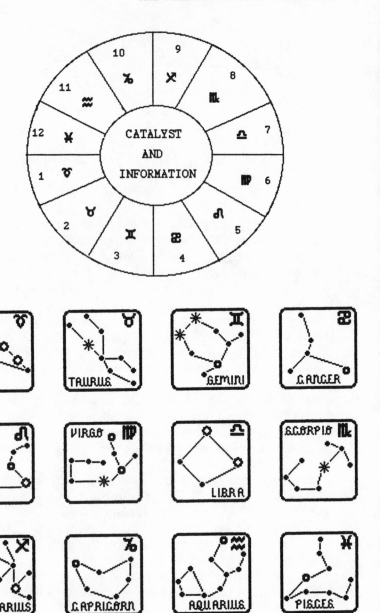

THE HOUSES OF THE ZODIAC

The Western System of astrology is composed of twelve (12) houses numbered from one (1) to twelve (12). Each house occupies 30 degrees of a zodiac circle and is identified by its own unique symbol. The identifying symbol is derived from an associated star constellation.

The houses are numbered in sequence from 1 to 12, as each house represents a natural progression of the incarnated soul. Beginning with house #1, Aries, the "New Soul" progresses through "New Beginnings" and proceeds through each house to house #12, Pisces, the house of the "Old Soul." Thus each house represents certain aspects of the soul's journey and subsequent mastering of life's lessons.

As you read through the descriptions of the twelve houses of the zodiac on the following pages, pay particular attention to which houses you might choose to help you in the construction of your first talisman.

For example, suppose you elect to make a money talisman. Pay particular attention then to the House of Taurus. Should the talisman be for love, consult the House of Leo.

Accompanying each astrological house description is a listing of fifteen different "associations" that will enable you to quickly determine which house is correct for the type of talisman you are creating. At the end of this chapter, a more detailed explanation of how to mix and match these associations will be given. These association explanations are for the more advanced student and also for those who wish to construct a more traditional talisman.

ASTROLOGICAL HOUSES

ARIES
First House (#1)
March 20 through April 19

ARIES
First House (#1)
March 20 through April 19

I AM

Key Words: Birth, newness, discovery, self-expression, the physical body.

Lessons: How to present yourself to the world in a non-threatening manner. How to be accepted. Self-trust.

Meanings: New beginnings and new lessons in life. Self-interest. Self-expression. Self-awareness. Your external appearance. How you are perceived and related to. Your career and job offers. All physical health. Your temperament, habits, behavior and personality.

Associations

Color: Bright Scarlet
Day: Tuesday
Metal: Iron
Element: Fire
Planet/Planetary Hour: Mars
Direction: South
Elemental: Salamanders
Symbol: Ram
Animals: All aggressive creatures of this and other worlds
Gems: Diamond, Fire Agate, and Bloodstone
Fragrance/Scent: All Spice, Carnation, Dragon's Blood, Ginger, High John the Conqueror, Honeysuckle, Peppermint, Pine, and Snapdragon
Parts of the Body: Blood (pressure), face, head, nerves, and sinuses
Plants: Bistort, Blessed Thistle, Bog Myrtle, Broom, Burdock, Cayenne, Cowslip, Fo Ti, Garlic, Gentian, Gotu Kola, Holy Thistle, Honeysuckle, Hops, Horse Radish, Hyacinth, Marjoram, Nettle, Red Clover, Rosemary, Salid Burnet, Sassafrass, St. Johns Wort, Yarrow, and Yellow Dock

Deities of Aries: Fire, Revenge, Power and Beauty

African and Haitian Voodoo

Goddess: Oshun—Beauty
God: Chango—Handsomeness

Angels

Camael/Sammael/Zamael: Rules Tuesday and Mars
Sarahiel: Rules Aries

Celtic-Welsh

Goddess: Macha—Patron and protector of females and female warriors. Strength and dominance over men in life and battle.
God: Llew—Governs fire, handsomeness, strength, revenge, skills of war and warriors.

China

Goddess: Tien-Hou—Fire, lightning, and storms.
God: Kuan Ti—Revenge, valor, justice, a warrior God.

Egypt

Goddess: Neith—Goddess of War—Governs all aspects of war, peace, arbitration and political affairs.
God: Horus—God of War—Governs all aspects of war, arbitration and politics. The avenging God.

Greece

Goddess: Artemis—Amazon War Goddess—Protector of Women.
God: Heracules-Heroism, good looks, power, strength, and courage.

India

Goddess: Durga—The Goddess of War, agility in battle and in the use of weapons; power and strength.

God: Agni—New beginnings, power, virility, and lightning.

Japan

Goddess: Amaterasu—Sun, warmth, beauty, Shintoism; the ruler of all deities.

God: Bishamon—God of War and patron of warriors and the skills of war.

Native and Latin America

Goddess: Huitzilopochtli—Goddess of all aspects of War and Fire.

God: Catequil—God of Fire and Lightning; a weapons expert, particularly the mace and sling.

Nordic-Germanic

Goddess: Alaisiagae—A War Goddess of the Valkyries.

God: Freyr—A Sun and Fire God; male virility and sensuality.

Oceania

Goddess: Pelé—Fire Goddess, growth through destruction.

God: Oro—God of War, all aspects.

Roman

Goddess: Mah-Bellonia—Governs war, diplomacy, military campaigns, defense, offense including the politics of war, and territorial sovereignty.

God: Hercules—Governs power, physical strength, courage, male charm, virility, and good looks.

Saint

Michael: To be victorious in wars, battles and conflicts.

TAURUS
Second House (#2)
April 21 through May 20

I ACQUIRE

Key Words: Money, freedom, earning opportunities, and personal resources.

Lessons: How to obtain from and succeed in, the material world.

Meanings: Your potential for acquiring the things you need and/or desire in life such as wealth, land, talent, and skill. The profits and losses from those needs and desires.

Associations

Colors: Greens and Browns
Day: Friday
Metal: Copper
Element: Earth
Planet/Planetary Hour: Venus
Direction: North
Elemental: Gnomes, Trolls and Hobbits
Symbol: Bull
Animals: Wild animals that are non-predatory by nature: Stag, bison, buffalo, ground squirrels, chipmunks, and rabbits
Gems: Emerald, Turquoise, Malachite, and Lapis Lazuli
Fragrance/Scent: African Violet, Cherry, Lilac, Primrose, Rose, Spearmint, Strawberry, Thyme, and Vanilla
Parts of the Body: Digestive tract, ears, excess emotions, larynx, neck, nose, throat and vocal cords.

Plants: Barberry, Cascara Sagrada, Camomile, Catmint, Coltsfoot, Comfrey, Elder Flower, Fenugreek, Garden Mint, Ginger, Goldenrod, Liccorice, Lovage, Papaya, Peppermint, Plantain, Sage, Silver Weed, Slippery Elm, Tansy, Thyme, Valeran

Deities of Taurus: Earth and Prosperity

African and Haitian Voodoo

Goddess: Yemaya Ataramagwa Sarabbi Olokun—Great wealth.

God: Babalu-Aye—Patron of wealth and prosperity.

Angels

Anael/Aniel: Rules Venus and Fridays.
Araziel/Asimodel: Rules Taurus.

Celtic-Welsh

Goddess: Ceridwen—Earth Mother
God: Cernunnos—Earth Father

China

Goddess: Kuan-Yin—Mother Goddess of success, abundance, and wealth in all areas of life.

God: Lu-Hsing—For success, prosperity. Governs all income from salaries.

Egypt

Goddess: Heqit—The Giver of the Gift of Abundance—The inventor of agriculture, commerce. Use for building wealth through honest dealings.

God: Hapi—Wealth and prosperity through trade and commerce via water.

Greece

Goddess: The Three Charities-Thalia (abundance), Euphrosyne (joy) and Aglaia (glory).
God: Boreas—Great riches, prosperity, and abundance.

India

Goddess: Gauri—Wealth and good fortune.
God: Kuvera—Governs all wealth and treasures buried within the earth.

Japan

Goddess: Benzaiten—Use in Taurus for abundance, wealth, good fortune, and prosperity.
God: Bishamon—Under Taurus, he guards and creates wealth. He can alter destiny to promote wealth.

Native and Latin America

Goddess: Chantico—The accumulator of wealth, precious stones, and minerals.
God: Pachacamac—The Patron of the worker and occupations.

Nordic-Germanic

Goddess: Nehallennia—Use for abundance and plenty in all aspects of life.
God: Freyr—Abundance, success, wealth, joy, and peace.

Oceania

Goddess: Humea—Efficient and effective productivity, especially when dealing in herbs.
God: Tane—Governs all aspects of craftsmanship and forestry, including the spiritual knowledge of each.

Roman

Goddess: Ops—Use for wealth, abundance and success.
God: Bonus—For success in any venture, enterprise, or undertaking regarding commerce and money matters.

Saint

Martha: For the necessities of life and everyday living.

GEMINI
Third House (#3)
May 21 through June 24

I COMMUNICATE

Key Words: Communications, siblings, short trips, vehicles.
Lessons: Learn to express one's self through communication and education.
Meanings: Mental plane. How you speak. Your immediate neighborhood, work area, and environment. Blood relatives and all with whom we have affection but do not live with. Mental clarity. Intellect, education, and science. All forms of communication and communications equipment. Short trips entailing walking or jogging.

Associations

Color: Yellow
Day: Wednesday
Metal: Quick Silver
Element: Air
Planet/Planetary Hour: Mercury
Direction: East
Elemental: Zephyrs and Sylphs

Symbol: Twins

Animals: Non-predatory birds as a whole, but primarily song birds

Gems: Amber, Pearl, Pyrites (Fool's Gold), Topaz, and Yellow Citrine

Fragrance/Scent: Azalea, Bayberry, Clover, Fern, Hemp, Lavender, Lemon Grass, Lilly of the Valley, Mandrake, Peppermint, and Tobacco

Parts of the Body: Arms, hands, lungs, mucous linings, nerves, and shoulders

Deities of Gemini: Wisdom

African and Haitain Voodoo

Goddess: Olukun (male or female). Use for obtaining knowledge of all secrets or mysteries.

God: Eleggua, the Messenger of Wisdom (his darker side is named Eshu Ogguanilebbe and represents the crafty, sinister, and mischievous wisdom).

Angels

Ambriel/Saraiel: Ruler of Gemini.

Michael: Ruler of Mercury and Wednesdays.

Celtic-Welsh

Goddess: Morgan—To obtain wisdom and knowledge of battles, magickal arts, revenge and prophecy.

God: Oghma—The God of alphabets, writing, reading, and literature.

China

Goddess: Kuan Yin, the All Knowing Mother. Under Gemini, she controls wisdom, patience, knowledge, and the secrets of enlightenment.

God: K'uei-Hsing—Patron of education, tests, literature, students. A protector of weary travelers.

Egypt

Goddess: Maat—Truth, wisdom, law, justice, and the final judgment of the soul.

God: Osiris—Initiation, priests, civilization, law, and justice.

Greece

Goddess: Athena—A feminist fighter for women's rights. She governs education, science, writing, and wisdom.

God: Hermes—Governs knowledge and cunning, a prankster.

India

Goddess: Aditi—Knows all. Teaches scrying to see the past, present and future.

God: Ganesa—Governs literature, writing, books, and wisdom.

Japan

Goddess: Benton—Governs literature, wisdom, reading, and comprehension.

God: Bishamon—Under Gemini, Bishamon is the patron of lawyers.

Native and Latin America

Goddess: Auchimalgen—The Messenger Goddess—She foretells of danger and warns of approaching death. She also banishes evil spirits.

God: Coyote or Raven—Both are cunning tricksters, intelligent with glib tongues and full of wisdom and knowledge.

Nordic-Germanic

Goddess: Freya—Under Gemini, Freya governs cunning, wisdom, and the ability to see beyond the illusion of life and death. A teacher of magick, knowledge, and power.

God: Loki—A wise and cunning God of deceit, lies and mischief making. He is the patron of dishonesty, destruction, and the criminal element.

Oceania

Goddess: Imberombera—Governs all aspects of language.
God: Aluluei—Governs knowledge of the sea.

Roman

Goddess: Minerva—A champion of women's rights, the law, writers, science, architectural knowledge, wisdom, intelligence, and medicine.
God: Mercury—A Messenger God governing speed, flying, wisdom, cunning, mischievousness, and intelligence.

Saint

Augustine: For wisdom.

CANCER
Fourth House (#4)
June 25 through July 23

I PERCEIVE

Key Words: Birth, Death, Endings, Family, Feelings, Home and Long Life.
Lessons: Learn to deal with emotion.
Meanings: Roots-ancestry, childhood, food, family, home town, inheritance, male relatives, and place of birth. Emotional security. Your deepest strengths. Possessions (buildings and land). Retirement (old age) or the conclusion of any matter.

Associations

Color: All shades of whites, cream pastels, pearlesques, and irradiant colors.

Day: Monday

Metal: Silver, White Gold, and Platinum

Element: Water

Planet/Planetary Hour: Moon

Direction: West

Elemental: Undines and Nymphs

Symbol: Crab

Animals: Water Mammals and mammals that dwell near the water. All water creatures that exit to land for short periods.

Gems: Chalcedony, Milk Opal, Moonstone, and White Serpentine

Fragrance/Scents: Balm, Coconut, Eucalyptus, Gardenia, Lotus, Myrrh, Poppy, Sandalwood, Water Lily, and Wintergreen

Parts of the Body: Breasts, digestive system, eyes, liver, and veins (varicose)

Deities of Cancer: Emotion

African and Haitian Voodoo

Goddess: Oba—Patroness of jilted women.

God: Eleggua—For power and protection of the home, none can oppose him.

Angels

Abuzhar: The angel of moon magick and invocations on Monday.

Muriel/Phakiel: Rules Cancer.

Celtic-Welsh

Goddess: The three aspects of the Moon Goddess-Danu, Dannanon and Morrigan, the protectors of all females from birth to the grave, in the house, in the family and home including all rites of passage. Governs women's mysteries and the three aspects of life as the Maiden, Mother, and Crone. Also governs fresh water from rain, lakes, rivers, and streams.

God: Bel—"The Great Father" governs emotions that are conflicting, cold or harsh. Also rules ice water from mountains, winter ice, and snow.

China

Goddess: Hsi Wang Mu—"Queen of the West" and of immortality.

God: Tsao-Wang—Governs cooking, the kitchen, hearth and the hearth fires. He protects the family home and all who dwell within.

Egypt

Goddess: Tefnut—The goddess of moisture, rain, dew and mist.

God: Haroeris—"God of the Moon." He governs moon magick and mysteries, water, emotions, and balance.

Greece

Goddess: Aphrodite—"Goddess of the Moon." She governs women's mysteries, old age, rites of passage, and emotional balance.

God: Eros—Under Cancer, Eros is the master of the emotions of love. Heterosexual, homosexual, and bisexual affairs are all within his power, which, frequently, creates love slaves or drives others to self sacrifice.

India

Goddess: Ganga—Governs fresh water and rivers.

God: Agni—Governs immortality, protects the home and controls the weather.

Japan

Goddess: Kishi-Mojin—She provides a balance in the home life, family, and women's mysteries.

God: Oki-Tsu-Hiko—A god of the kitchen and cooking.

Native and Latin America

Goddess: Chantico—Governs the home and hearth, the pleasure and pain of life. Controls the rites of passage, heals emotions, and aids in a family crisis.

God: Aulanerk—The god of tides and waves. He brings happiness, plenty, and joy.

Nordic-Germanic

Goddess: Bertha—The Hag who rules winter and the winter of life. The rites of passage into later life along with the respect and position that elders hold in the family.

God: Heimdall—He signifies the twilight of life for men and gods alike.

Oceania

Goddess: Imberombera-Hina—A goddess of the moon and women's mysteries.

God: Kamapua—A water god of the mist, fog and rain. A god of shape shifting and mystery who uses the weather to cloak or disguise himself.

Roman

Goddess: Juno—Juno protects women, children, home, family, and the aged from danger, evil, and misfortune.

God: Saturn—In Cancer, Saturn controls the lessons and treatments received in the golden years of life.

Saint

Mary Magdalene: Caring for others.

LEO

LEO
Fifth House (#5)
July 24 through August 22

I EXPERIENCE

Key Words: Arts, children, crafts, love affairs, romance, and risks.

Lessons: To experience life with its many wonders through creative expression.

Meanings: Love of acting, adventure, beverage, children, creating, expression, gambling, life, love affairs, love making, luxury, recreation, risks, romance, theater, sex, singing, speculation, and sports.

Associations

Color: Orange
Day: Sunday
Metal: Gold (usually mixed with copper).
Element: Fire
Planet/Planetary Hour: Sun
Direction: South
Elemental: Salamanders
Symbol: Lion
Animals: All creatures that use, in some form, tools and have developed a limited ability to count, think and build . . . i.e Apes, Beavers, Crows, and Monkeys
Gems: Madera Citrine, Peridot, Red Carnelian, and Sun Stone
Fragrance/Scent: Cedar, Chrysanthemum, Cinnamon, Cloves, Frankincense, Juniper, Marigold, Rosemary, Rowan, and Rue
Parts of the Body: Back (upper), circulatory system (weak), and heart

Deities of Leo: The Family

African and Haitian Voodoo

Goddess: Oya—The patroness of love and pleasure. She governs mistresses, cheating wives, and lovers.

God: Olokun—Patron of hermaphrodites and sexual orientation, either mental or physical.

Angels

Seratiel/Verchiel: Rules Leo.
Raphael: Rules the Sun and Sundays.

Celtic-Welsh

Goddess: Brigid—Governs the feminine arts which include arts, crafts, love making, poetry, romance, and sensuality. She also controls all female wiles and cunning in matters of love and love magick.

God: Luga Lamfada—The inventor and master of all skills using the hands; builders, cultural arts, crafts, masonry, music, and metal smiths (precious).

China

Goddess: Chih-Nii—Governs the craft of spinners, cloth and cloth making.

God: Lupan—The god of artists and craftsmen.

Egypt

Goddess: Bast—Governs all of the pleasures of the flesh, singing, and dancing.

God: Khnem—Governs all arts and crafts requiring skill.

Greece

Goddess: The Nine Muses—Calliope, Clio, Erato, Euterpe, Melpomene, Polyhymnia, Terpsichore, Thalia, Urania.

God: Eros—Under Leo, love is the art of Eros, whether homosexual, heterosexual, or bisexual. All art of the acts of pleasure is within his realm.

India

Goddess: Shakti—The goddess of beauty, bliss, and sexual ecstasy. Gentle and loving, she governs sexuality and sensuality. She teaches the mysteries of Tantra and eternal youth.

God: Tvashtar—The patron of craftsmen. He teaches skill for handicraft and labor.

Japan

Goddess: Uzume—The goddess of bawdy conduct and language, especially centered on acting and entertainment that includes singing, merriment, and dancing (primarily striptease).

God: Susanowo—The patron of mischievousness, exuberance and immaturity in all aspects of life.

Native and Latin America

Goddess: Anka—Governs childbirth, feminine wiles, arts, and crafts.

God: Shakuru—"God of the Sun Dance."

Nordic-Germanic

Goddess: Freya—In Leo, she governs beauty, love, the arts, and feminine charm and wiles.

God: Bragi—Governs the masculine eloquence of music, poetry, wit, and charm.

Oceania

Goddess: Pelé—In Leo, Pelé is hot and fiery. She governs feminine wiles and jealousy. She is wild and free, possessive and demanding. She is the insatiable lover that can never be possessed.

God: Tilitr—The patron of music, singing, and magickal chants.

Roman

Goddess: Minerva—In Leo, Minerva governs the creative arts and craftsmanship.

God: Fanus—An advocate of male sexuality that includes song, dance, merriment, and drink.

Saint

Teresa of Avila: For a sense of humor and good humor.

VIRGO
Sixth House (#6)
August 23 through September 22

I SERVE

Key Words: Animals (small), health, and service.

Lessons: Enjoying the performance of your work, obligations and commitments.

Meanings: Your job and/or career in any of the service fields . . . i.e. domestic, food, health, hygiene, military, nutrition. Self improvement. Self sacrifice.

Associations

Color: Mixed colors of pale yellows and baby blues.
Day: Friday
Metal: All mixed alloys
Element: Earth
Planet/Planetary Hour: Mercury
Direction: Northeast
Elemental: Zephyrs, Sylphs, Gnomes, Trolls, and Hobbits
Symbol: Goddess of the Harvest
Animals: Flying mammals

Gems: Multicolored Fluorite-Pastels, Sapphire, and Watermelon Turmaline

Fragrance/Scent: Azalea, Bayberry, Clover, Fern, Hemp, Lavender, Lemon Grass, Lily of the Valley, Mandrake, Peppermint, and Tobacco

Parts of the Body: Digestive organs, and nerves

Deities of Virgo: Service

African and Haitian Voodoo

Goddess: Ayé—The goddess of midgets and small people in general.

God: Aroni—Governs medicine and medical treatment.

Angels

Hamaliel/Schaltiel: Rules Virgo.

Michael: Rules Mercury and Wednesdays.

Celtic-Welsh

Goddess: Morgan—The patron of Green Witches and priestesses who act as healers and midwives.

God: Llew—Patron of physicians and healers.

China

Goddess: Pi-Hsaia-Yuan-Chun—In Virgo, she protects women and children from evil and danger.

God: Shui-Kuan—In Virgo, he dispels and averts evil, defends and protects men.

Egypt

Goddess: Bast—Governs the secrets of healing disease, especially with psychic energy.

God: Imhotep—Governs the knowledge of medicine and healing.

Greece

Goddess: Aphrodite—Governs herbal and healing magick.

God: Asclepius—Governs healing, medicine, and medical care.

India

Goddess: Shakti—She heals the soul and makes whole those that are sexually inadequate, inept, frustrated, and incomplete.

God: Rudra—He teaches the healing of disease through the use of herbs. He governs the use of and the secrets of all jungle and woodland plants.

Japan

Goddess: Kishi-Mojin—"The Universal Mother." All secrets of the healing arts are known to her.

God: Okuninushi—He governs healing, medicine, and cunning sorcery that is used for banishing evil disease causing spirits.

Native and Latin America

Goddess: Xochiquetzal—Governs the secret powers of flowers and how to use them.

God: Loskeha—Governs the ritual use of the sacred tobacco with regard to the healing of disease.

Nordic-Germanic

Goddess: Freya—In Virgo, Freya is the mistress of cats. She possesses an incredible knowledge and power regarding herbs, healing, and magick.

God: Odin—Governs healing and magickal powers as taught to him by Freya.

Oceania

Goddess: Haumea—Wild plants and their use in healing.

God: Tane—Governs the secret power of forest and jungle plants and their use in healing.

Roman

Goddess: Venus—Governs the secrets of love and herbal magick.

God: Helios—Governs the knowledge and skill within the medicinal arts and herbology.

Saint

Bernadette: For healing the body of disease.

LIBRA
Seventh House (#7)
September 23 through October 22

I HARMONIZE

Key Words: Contracts, Divorce, Enemies, Lawsuits, Marriages, Opposition, Partnerships.

Lessons: How you relate to yourself and the world around you; learning to co-operate.

Meanings: Relationships, friendships, partnerships, relatives, and spouses. How you relate to and react to public officials. Your interaction with regard to divorce, fornication, marriage, and prostitution.

Associations

Color: Pale yellows, sky blues, soft pinks, lime greens and soft browns
Day: Wednesday
Metal: Copper mixed with gold
Element: Air
Planet/Planetary Hour: Venus
Direction: Northeast
Elemental: Zephyrs and Sylphs
Symbol: The Scales of Justice
Animals: Predatory birds
Gems: Aquamarine, Clear quartz crystal, Opal, and Sapphire
Fragrance/Scent: African Violet, Cherry, Fern, Hemp, Lavender, Lemon Grass, Lily of the Valley, Mandrake, Peppermint, and Tobacco
Parts of the Body: Back (lower), kidneys, nerves, ovaries, skin (ailments), and veins

Deities of Libra: Others

African and Haitian Voodoo

Goddess: Nzambi—Rewards the good done by all, but also punishes the evil as well.
God: Chiyidi—Creates nightmares to torment enemies.

Angels

Abael/Aniel/Haniel: Rules Venus and Fridays
Chadakiel/Zuriel: Rules Libra

Celtic-Welsh

Goddess: Banba—Repels open enemies and attacking invaders.
God: Nuada—Champions those in danger from open enemies.

China

Goddess: Tien-Hou—Protects anyone who is in danger.
God: Sung-Chiang—Patron of mischief makers, thieves, and thievery.

Egypt

Goddess: Selket—Patroness of happy marriages, enjoyable sex and free sexuality within marriage.
God: Bes—Protects from demons, animals, and evil that stalk the night.

Greece

Goddess: Selene—Governs brides, the marriage bed, and the secrets of pleasure on the wedding night.
God: Zeus—In Libra, Zeus defends the weak and helpless. Protects the friendships and associations with others. Oversees aspects of justice and the law.

India

Goddess: Tara—A compassionate goddess who breaks up illusions for clear seeing and understanding. She can judge and dispense justice harshly and swiftly.
God: Puchan—He will guide those who inquire into marriage, wealth, and business success.

Japan

Goddess: Kishimo-Jin—Protects women, children, childbirth, and the home from enemies and bad luck.
God: Jizo Bosatsu—Protects men, women, children, the dead, and women in labor from any evil that may be lurking about.

Native and Latin America

Goddess: Ataentsic—Governs marriage and the duties required of a wife. She offers help in all aspects of married life.

God: Nohochacyum—Defends all who call against evil and enemies.

Nordic-Germanic

Goddess: Freya—In Libra, use Freya as a protection goddess via magickal intervention.
God: Thor—A protector via physical intervention.

Oceania

Goddess: Imberombera—Governs the secrets of peace, living in harmony, the wisdom of nature, intelligence, and common sense in all actions.
God: Oro—Possesses the knowledge of war, politics, negotiations, and the peace making process.

Roman

Goddess: Minerva—In Libra, Minerva governs the laws concerning women and their rights.
God: Apollo—A god of law and order, justice served.

Saint

Agia: Lawsuits.

SCORPIO
Eighth House (#8)
October 23 through November 22

I TRANSFORM

Key Words: Death, debts, inheritance, money and goods of a partner or others, taxes, the occult, sex.
Lessons: Transformation.

Meanings: Your ability to experience and/or deal with birth, death or transcendence; spiritual regeneration, and occult studies; deep emotion and physical upheaval; catastrophes; sexual relations including perversity, sexual magick, rape, and incest.

Legal matters dealing with estates, inheritances, taxes, undertakers, executors, insurances, wills, and dowries.

Associations

Color: Dark ruby reds
Day: Saturday
Metal: Lead and plutonium
Element: Water
Planet/Planetary Hour: Mars (emphasis fire) or Pluto (emphasis earth)
Direction: Southwest for Mars, Northwest for Pluto
Elemental: Nymphs, salamanders and Undines (water) or Gnomes, Hobbits, Nymphs, Trolls, and Undines (earth)
Symbol: Scorpion or Eagle
Animals: All creatures that live between realities. Creatures of legend
Gems: Black tourmaline, Obsidian, Opal, Topaz, and Tourmalated quartz
Fragrance/Scent: *Mars*: All Spice, Carnation, Dragons Blood, Ginger, High John the Conqueror, Honeysuckle, Peppermint, Pine, and Snapdragon. *Pluto*: Ambergris, Damania, Dragons Blood, Eucalyptus, False Unicorn Root, Foxglove, Ground Pine, Hops, Kava, Musk, Oats, Orchid Root, Rye, Wheat, and Yucca.
Parts of the Body: Bladder, circulatory system, elimination organs, heart, muscular system, reproductive/sex organs, and urinary tract.

Deities of Scorpio: Seeking

African and Haitian Voodoo

Goddess: Maman Brigitte—Governess of death and the death rites, all mysteries, life itself, regeneration, and licentiousness.

God: Eshu Ogguanilebbe—Governs accidents, corners, crossroads, doors, violent death. The patron of killers.

Angels

Barbiel/Barchiel/Sartzeil: Rules Scorpio.
Camael/Sammael/Zamael: Rules Mars and Tuesdays.

Celtic-Welsh

Goddess: Blodwin—Either opens or closes the gates of regeneration, annihilation, death, life, panic, and terror at will.
God: Dagda—Governs life and death.

China

Goddess: Pi-Hsaia-Yuan-Chun—In Scorpio, she is the patroness of newborns and mothers in labor or actually giving birth.
God: Chu-Jung—The God of Revenge. He enforces karma and karmic justice.

Egypt

Goddess: Selket—Governs sexual pleasure in marriage. A protector and guide for the departed soul after death.
God: Anubis—Governs embalming and tombs and acts as a guide and protector for the dead.

Greece

Goddess: Demeter—Governs rebirth, renewal, reincarnation, and all rites of passage.
God: Asclepius—Governs the revival of the dead and the mastery over death.

India

Goddess: Kali-Ma—The patroness of magick, witches, revenge, destruction, death, and reincarnation.
God: Manjusri—The Annihilator, the lord of death who also teaches science, enlightenment, and civilization.

Japan

Goddess: Amaterasu—Governs life, death, rebirth, and regeneration.

God: Emma-O—Rules the nether world of death. He rules over death and destruction.

Native and Latin America

Goddess: Huitzilopochtli—"The Death Goddess," all aspects of.

God: Aipaloovic—The god of corruption, murder, vice, vandalism, scandal, and destruction. He knows the secrets of all. He is best used to uncover evil doers.

Nordic-Germanic

Goddess: Valkyries—They are the protectors and guides for both men and women warriors into Valhalla.

God: Wodan—Governs reincarnation, death, and the restless spirits of men slain and unable to reach Valhalla.

Oceania

Goddess: Pelé—In Scorpio, Pelé governs the human temper, death, violence, destruction, revenge, and dark magick.

God: Atea—Holds the secrets of regenerating the life force with anything.

Roman

Goddess: Ceres—The goddess who governs reincarnation, initiation, renewal, and all mysteries dealing with death.

God: Saturn—In Scorpio, Saturn is the time and record keeper of the past, present, and future of life. He governs the karmic lessons, blocks, obstacles, and other problems faced in this incarnation.

Saint

Holy Rosary: To avert and conquer misfortune.

SAGITTARIUS
Ninth House (#9)
November 23 through December 22

I THEORIZE

Key Words: Godself, In-laws, Long journeys, Magick, and Philosophical and Law Professions.

Lessons: The discovery of one's own inner self, divinity and power.

Meanings: Spiritual evolution and travel. Embarking on crusades involving martyrdom and self-sacrifice. Seeking the God or Goddess within. Long journeys seeking higher education regarding spiritual growth, philosophical endeavors, religious understandings, divination, dreams, and anything of an esoteric nature.

Associations

Color: Red or bluish purple
Day: Thursday
Metal: Tin
Element: Fire
Planet/Planetary Hour: Jupiter
Direction: Southeast
Elemental: Salamander
Symbol: Archer or Centaur
Animals: Large animals or birds that thrive in hot climates
Gems: Magnetite, Purple Fluorite, Termilated quartz, and Turquoise
Fragrance/Scent: Anise, Datura, Lime, Magnolia, Maple, Meadowsweet, Nutmeg, Oak, Sage, and Sandalwood
Parts of the Body: Arteries, hips, joints, and thighs

Deities of Sagittarius: Experiencing

African and Haitian Voodoo

Goddess: Ayizan—The goddess of ancestral magick and power.

God: Ifa—Governs divination and the knowledge of all time.

Angels

Advachiel/Adnachiel/Saritiel: Rules Sagittarius.
Zachariel/Zadkiel: Rules Jupiter and Thursday.

Celtic-Welsh

Goddess: Morrighan—Governs battlefields, death, enchantments, female shape shifters, fresh water, magick, psychic abilities, priestesses, prophecy, sorcery, the night, and witches.

God: Merlin—Governs divination, psychic abilities, rituals, spells, and incantations.

China

Goddess: Kuan-Yin—In Sagittarius, she governs enlightenment and spiritual evolution.

God: Yao-Shih—Governs the controlling and learning of E.S.P.

Egypt

Goddess: Nebthet—The darker sister of Isis who governs all secrets of dark magick and knowledge.

God: Ra—Governs the secrets of ritual magick and the performance of spells.

Greece

Goddess: Circe—The goddess of shape shifting, love magick, enchantments, talismans, vengeance, witchcraft, and the protection of women through guile.

God: Dactyls—Governs the secrets of creating magickal formulae.

India

Goddess: Shakti—Governs wisdom, understanding, magick, and the proper use of energy.

God: Shiva—Male counterpart of Shakti.

Japan

Goddess: Uzume—Controls the secrets of ancient shamanism; magick through chant, song, dance, trance, and meditations.

God: O-Kuni-Nushi—Governs the arts of sorcery and healing.

Native and Latin America

Goddess: Spider Woman, Witches, The Hag or The Crone aspect of the Triple Goddess. All aspects of magick dealing with the dark side of the moon.

God: Michabo—Governs magick of all types, inventions, and shape shifting.

Nordic-Germanic

Goddess: Freya—In Sagittarius, all types of magick, enchantments, spells, sorcery and power are her secrets and within her ability to teach.

God: Odin—It is said that Odin obtained his power and knowledge in magick from the teachings of Freya.

Oceania

Goddess: Pelé—In Sagittarius, Pelé governs shape shifting and the secrets of female power and force.

God: Maui—Governs all aspects of mischief in magick, sorcery, shape shifting, and charms.

Roman

Goddess: Diana—Governs magick, sorcery, enchantments and witchcraft, and all matter of psychic abilities.
God: Vulcan—Governs metallurgy and magick.

Saint

Our Lady of Fatima: Riches on a spiritual level.

CAPRICORN
Tenth House (#10)
December 23 through January 20

I REALIZE

Key Words: Advancement, fame, honor, power, and relations with authorities.
Lessons: Learning to achieve acceptance in the world and to assess your own worth.
Meanings: Discovering your own personal power and your relationships with those in authority over you. Determine your own goals, discover your destiny, enhance your ambition, status, honor, recognition, and reputation.

Associations

Color: Black and all other very dark colors.
Day: Saturday
Metal: Lead
Element: Earth
Planet/Planetary Hour: Saturn
Direction: North
Elemental: Gnomes, Hobbits, and Trolls

Symbol: Goat or Sea Goat

Animals: Any animal including birds, fish, and insects, that live within a stratified social structure

Gems: Azurite, Garnet, Indicolite, and Tourmaline

Fragrance/Scent: Black Orchid, Hyacinth, Iris, Opium Poppy, Pansy, Patchouly, Peyote, and Solomon's Seal

Parts of the Body: Bones, circulation, ears, eyes, heart, knees, liver, nerves, and teeth

Deities of Capricorn: Reputation

African and Haitian Voodoo

Goddess: Oduddua—The Mother Goddess; all power and authority.

God: Obatala—The Father God; all power and authority.

Angels

Semaqiel: Rules Capricorn.

Kafziel/Orifiel: Rules Saturn and Saturday.

Celtic-Welsh

Goddess: Danu—The Mother Goddess of magick, mortals, and goddesses. The all knowing and powerful giver of abundance, happiness, and plenty.

God: Dagda—The Father God of the heavens, magick, mortals, and gods. The all knowing and powerful dispenser of discipline, life, and death.

China

Goddess: Kuan-Yin—The Mother Goddess of compassion and mercy. She dissolves hardships and fear within the lives of those who call upon her.

God: Tai-Yueh-Ta-Ti—Dispenses great honor and favor, in the eyes of others, upon the seeker.

Egypt

Goddess: Isis—The Supreme Mother; the patroness of priestesses. Governs knowledge and successful endeavors.

God: Ammon—The Father God of Agriculture.

Greece

Goddess: Hecate—An incredibly powerful Mother Goddess. Success in any area of endeavor is within her realm.

God: Zeus—In Capricorn, Zeus is the Great Father God who defends those unable to defend themselves. Honors, riches and health, almost anything the heart might desire is within the power of Zeus in Capricorn.

India

Goddess: Aditi—The Mother of Space and all Gods. She is the cosmos, the Unmanifest, Chaos, the Unborn, and the Order. She controls the fate and destiny of all things. She gave birth to the twelve Spirits of the Zodiac.

God: Brama—The Father of the Gods, animals, men, and the universe. He imparts knowledge and wisdom.

Japan

Goddess: Izanami—The Creative Mother Goddess who gave birth to all creation.

God: Izanagi—The Father God of all creation.

Native and Latin America

Goddess: Coatlicue—The Great Mother Goddess, all knowing and all powerful. She aids in all areas of life, growth, and prosperity.

God: Viracocho—The Great Father God, all knowing and all powerful. He aids in all areas of life, growth, and prosperity.

Nordic-Germanic

Goddess: Vanadis—The Ruling Ancestor before patriarchy and Odin. An all knowing and all powerful goddess of boundless attributes and abilities.

God: Odin—The Father God of the sky, war, magick, justice, law, runes, weapons, arts, and the weather.

Oceania

Goddess: Imberombera—The Creation Goddess.

God: Great Rainbow Snake—He/she animates all life, bisexual.

Roman

Goddess: Ceres—The Eternal Mother of civilization and agriculture; all knowing and giving.

God: Jupiter—The Supreme Father of agriculture, fame, and riches; all knowing and giving.

Saint

Theresa of Lisieux: To obtain the ability of loving everyone.

AQUARIUS
Eleventh House (#11)
January 21 through February 20

I DREAM

Key Words: Circumstances seemingly beyond one's control. Cleansing and healing. Income from occupation. Love received. Social groups.

Lessons: Learning to create your own reality with you in total control.

Meanings: To influence friends, lovers, and publishers. Any connections with social life, peer groups, and patronage by the rich. Reforms and revolutions. Dealings with humanitarianism, ideals, and aspirations. Seeking beyond the material, mental, and spiritual planes.

Associations

Color: Dark electric blue.
Day: Saturday
Metal: Lead
Element: Air
Planet/Planetary Hour: Saturn (Earth) and/or Uranus (Air)—Metal: zinc
Direction: North or Northeast (your choice)
Elemental: Gnomes, Hobbits, and Trolls
Symbol: Water Bearer
Animals: Any creature that gathers or bands together into social groups for protection or survival
Gems: Amethyst, Black Fire Opal, Diamond, and Opalized Tourmaline
Fragrance/Scent: *Saturn*: Black Orchid, Hyacinth, Iris, Morning Glory, Opium Poppy, Pansy, Patchouly, Peyote and Solomon's Seal. *Uranus*: Coffee, Elfwort, Ginseng, Kola Nut, Linseed, Mandrake, Nutmeg, Pomegranate, True Unicorn root, Woody Nightshade
Parts of the Body: Ankles, calves, and legs

Deities of Aquarius: Aspirations

African and Haitian Voodoo

Goddess: The Erzulies, astral Amazons who fight for reforms and liberation.

God: Ogun, the God who removes obstacles and blocks, allowing easier progress in all life's goals and aspirations.

Angels

Cambiel/Gambiel/Tzakmaqiel: Rules Aquarius
Kafziel/Orifiel/Zaphiel: Rules Saturn and Saturday.

Celtic-Welsh

Goddess: Tailtiu—Call on to obtain peaceful circumstances and prosperity in an otherwise hopeless situation.

God: Sucellus—He who brings success to any situation that otherwise seems hopeless.

China

Goddess: Kuan-Yin—Use her in Aquarius for compassion and mercy. She dissolves hardships and fear that block the path of achievement, peace, and ultimate happiness.

God: Lei-King—He who dispenses justice, retribution, and karma to those who have escaped mortal law, thus fulfilling the hopes and pleas for justice by the innocent.

Egypt

Goddess: Renenet—The giver of fate and future upon incarnation.

God: Shait—The controller of destiny and fate.

Greece

Goddess: Themis—She who deals with the social; order of gatherings and the collective consciousness or unconsciousness of any group (three or more), organization, city, state, or nation.

God: Asclepius—Commands dreams and visions.

India

Goddess: Shakti—The provider of peace, comfort, love, and harmony. She replaces fear and anxiety when called upon. She also transmutes weakness into strength and happiness.

God: Agni—He who cleanses and purifies; offers peace, comfort, and forgiveness to those who seek it.

Japan

Goddess: Amaterasu—Use here for peace, happiness, compassion, and goodness.

God: Bishamon—Under Aquarius, he controls and teaches how to manipulate fate and destiny.

Native and Latin America

Goddess: Auchimalgen—She who banishes evil spirits or thoughtforms that cause doubt, fear, depression, and bad luck.

God: Bochicha—Controls all aspects of civilization; dealing with others in a civilized manner.

Nordic-Germanic

Goddess: Nerthus—The bringer of peace, harmony, balance, and success in overcoming fears or obstacles where concerns of wealth, fertility, and witchcraft are present.

God: Loki—In Aquarius, Loki reveals, thwarts and reverses the obnoxious plans or traps of others that endanger your hopes, goals, and social affairs.

Oceania

Goddess: Iberombera—In this house, she brings peace, prosperity, tranquility to family, civilization while aiding in communicating effectively with others.

God: Gidja—Controls and manifests the world of dreams, hopes, and fears.

Roman

Goddess: Fortuna—The Goddess of fate, chance, and all circumstances beyond the normal scope of control.

God: Jupiter—Under Aquarius, Jupiter fulfills dreams, hopes, and desires of the heart.

Saint

The Holy Rosary: Use to prevent being defeated by misfortune.

PISCES
Twelfth House (#12)
February 21 through March 19

I COMPLETE

Key Words: Secret enemies, large animals, all confinements, limitations, and worries.

Lessons: Facing the world alone and surviving.

Meanings: Unnecessary karmic lessons and bonds. Secret dreams, fears, hopes, and wishes. That which is hidden, the unseen or unexpected. The collective unconscious. Your relationship to the roles and structure of society. Self destruction, seclusion, betrayal, and loss. Past lives and the realization of one's own immortality. Plots, secret enemies, spies, intrigue, and mysterious illnesses.

Associations

Color: Royal blues and purples
Day: Thursday
Metal: Tin
Element: Water
Planet/Planetary Hour: Jupiter or Neptune (water)
Direction: East or West
Elemental: Nymphs, Sylphs, and Undines
Symbol: Two fish
Animal: Any large water mammal or fish
Gems: Bloodstone, Coral, Mother of Pearl, and Pearl
Fragrance/Scent: *Jupiter:* Agrimony, Burr Reed, Burdock, Chervil, Chicory, Dandelion, Horsetail, Houseleek, Mandrake,

Oak, Oregon Grape Root, Red Clover, Rock Rose, Sage, Scabius, Solomon's Seal, and Wild Yam *Neptune*: Adam and Eve Root, Balmony, Citrus, Lobelia, Lotus, Mescal, Narcissus, Passion Flower, Wild Hemp, Wild Lettuce, Wild Sage, and Wisteria
Parts of the Body: Chest, feet, joints (rheumatic), and toes

Deities of Pisces: Limitations

African and Haitian Voodoo

Goddess: Oyé—Blocks and confinements.
God: Ochosi—Imprisonment and confinements.

Angels

Barakiel/Barchiel/Vocatiel: Rules Pisces.
Zachariel/Zadkiel: Rules Jupiter and Thursdays.

Celtic-Welsh

Goddess: Epona—Rules all aspects of caring, healing, and taming of domestic or wild horses.
God: Nuada—He who champions those endangered from hidden enemies.

China

Goddess: Tien-Hou—The Patroness of sailors and anyone in danger.
God: Yueh-Ta-Ti—The protector of animals and men.

Egypt

Goddess: Isis—Under Pisces, Isis dispels fears, gives protection and abundance, solves mysteries, and reveals secrets.
God: Ptah—Use to transcend blocks and problems with creative power and begin anew.

Greece

Goddess: Hecate—Use Hecate in Pisces to break through trouble, fear, and obstacles.

God: Eros—In Pisces, Eros can create or destroy blinding self sacrifice.

India

Goddess: Tara—Banishes fear, especially the fear of death. She teaches self mastery and the exploration of the inner self.

God: Ganesa—Removes obstacles from life.

Japan

Goddess: Izanami—As the Goddess of Evil as well as Good, she is a Goddess of the nether world who can promote or banish all evils and ills that plague the human race.

God: Sae-No-Kam—Protects males from any misfortune they may encounter, especially on the road or during travel.

Native and Latin America

Goddess: Mama Quilla—A protector of women, especially married ones.

God: Kurupira—A Gnomelike God who protects animals and vegetation from abuse and danger.

Nordic-Germanic

Goddess: Holda—She can alter fate, karma and misfortune. She also destroys enemies while exposing danger or debauchery.

God: Alegir—A patron saint of sailors. He controls all aspects dealing with the sea.

Oceania

Goddess: Hina—Banishes and controls all that causes fear, nightmares, trauma, and unrest in life. She can dispatch hidden enemies and avert danger.

God: Tinirau—The Master of Oceans and Seas—All sea creatures are under his rule. Whales and sharks are used as his messengers.

Roman

Goddess: Prosperpina—Use her for survival. She breaks down obstacles and blocks, and defeats hidden enemies while making one victorious in the face of incredible odds.

God: Neptune—The God of the Sea—also controls fresh water and ships, horses, and bulls.

Saint

The Holy Rosary: For special protection.

Chapter 3 Quiz

1. Which two astrological houses are best for controlling dreams?
2. Which two houses are best for controlling enemies?
3. Which house is best to use to influence those in power over you?
4. Which house deals with death and taxes?
5. Which house controls wealth and abundance?

Answers

1. Aquarius (nightmare) and Sagittarius (send a dream).
2. Pisces (hidden enemies) and Libra (open enemies).
3. Capricorn.
4. Scorpio.
5. Taurus.

4

How to use Zodiac Associations to Create Talismans

As presented earlier, there are fifteen different associations listed under each of the twelve Zodiac Houses. When several of these associations are used in combination, they create a talisman representing the attributes of the parent house.

In the creation of a talisman for money, using the House of Taurus, which rules over money matters, you would apply the information found in the associations listed under Taurus as indicated below. Of course, the methods illustrated would apply to all other Zodiac Houses as well.

Color: The first association is color. Therefore in creating a talisman for Taurus or anything under the rulership of Taurus, the colors green and brown can be safely used.

Day: The next association would be the day most favorable for starting your talisman magick. For Taurus, you would begin on Friday during the hour of Venus.

Metal: Determine what metal, if any, you would use in your talisman construction. In this case, since we are using Taurus as an example, you would use pure copper.

At this point you are probably wondering why you would use pure copper instead of gold or silver. The answer lies in the fact that copper is the metal of Taurus, the money ruler, while gold is the metal of Leo. Leo is the house of fun and birth, not money. As you advance in your knowledge, you will eventually learn to create talismans that use both houses so that you can "give birth to money," but for now, let us stay with a one house talisman.

Elements: Everyone usually agrees that the world contains at least four elements; Earth, Air, Fire, and Water. Each of these elements has individual characteristics that are important in magick and talisman construction. In other words, you know that Taurus may have a planet that rules dominant with that house, but this domination is secondary to the ruling element Earth.

However cryptic or foreign this may seem to you at first, do not dismay. All this means is that Taurus, first of all, is very grounded and materialistic; while its secondary attribute is loving and good natured, the attributes of its ruling planet, Venus.

This explanation may be imparting information you are already familiar with, but there is a good reason for this. The more you begin to think in occult terms and to use occult logic, and begin to really understand why something is or why something works, the less memorization of seemingly endless terms and concepts you will have to undertake. It is only by understanding the logic behind the action that you quickly advance beyond the novice stage and begin to develop a natural feel for magickal work. Now, let us briefly discuss the four elements.

Earth: Earth governs all physical needs, comforts, and pleasures while in your present incarnation.

Air: Air governs anything to do with intelligence, thought, and communication.

Fire: Fire governs the temper, action, and aggression. Its primary function is to transmute or change whatever it comes into contact with.

Water: Water is the emotional world and the inner nature of each of us. It governs secrets and that which is hidden from view.

Ruling Planet: As previously mentioned, the ruling planet is secondary to the ruling element. It is by combining these two that you can get a more accurate and thorough understanding of the meanings and attributes of each zodiac house.

The planetary symbols themselves can be used singularly, or in combination, to create talismans composed entirely of planets. They are also assigned to various hours of the day and evening for performing magickal work.

By becoming familiar with the planets and their meanings, you will begin to appreciate which hour of the day or night is best for your magick. You will also come to realize how you can use the planets to influence each other in order to create more complicated talismans. Here is a brief and simple guide to the attributes ascribed to each of the planets.

Sun: Innocent, childlike, fun loving, irresponsible, and reckless, The Sun is used to begin new projects and to govern men's mysteries and magick.

Mercury: Education and thinking. To analyze and to communicate effectively.

Venus: Loving, gentle, creative, and compassionate. Venus is used primarily in all matters of creative endeavor and of the heart.

Moon: The Moon governs women's mysteries and magick. Receptive and intuitive, this is the planet of the gentle and loving mother (includes fathers/males who identify with these same qualities).

Mars: Physical and athletic competitions, sports, and all forms of aggression. The Amazon, the Warrior, both offensive and defensive.

Jupiter: Expansion and growth. Business/businessmen, politics/politicians, employers, and those others who are older and/or in power over you.

Saturn: Saturn deals with difficulties, blocks, obstructions, bureaucrats, and most anything that creates frustration or obstacles in your life.

Uranus: Scientists, inventors, and anything to do with modern day electrical or mechanical wizardry.

Neptune: The planet of the Mystics, Magickans, Witches, Sorcerers, and Spiritualists. The planet of discovery, leading to the inner and higher self.

Pluto: The transformer, the keeper of the secrets of life and death. Pluto governs large groups, obsessions, possessions, and corruption, along with the mysterious things that go bump in the night.

HOW THE PLANETS AFFECT A ZODIAC HOUSE

Continuing to use Taurus, the zodiac house for wealth as our example, let us quickly explore how each house would influence Taurus. In the house of Taurus, Venus is the primary and ruling planet. Any other planet placed within this house would become secondary to Venus' influences. Venus, "the love of . . ." would dominate any other planetary influence.

Sun: To create (Sun) wealth (Earth) and enjoy (Venus) the benefits therefrom.

Mercury: Knowledge of how to obtain (Mercury) money (Earth) and enjoy it (Venus).

Venus: To double up on Venus within this house creates not a state of love toward wealth (Earth) but an obsession, and, for that reason, is not recommended. The miser or money monger, someone who cannot get enough, would be created.

Moon: Emotional security (Moon) through wealth (Earth) and the enjoyment (Venus) it brings.

Mars: An individual's love (Venus) for a physical activity (Mars) has now become his or her profession and monetary means of support (Earth).

Jupiter: Jupiter simply amplifies what already is in existence. In this case, the love (Venus) and enjoyment of money (Earth) is enlarged (Jupiter).

Saturn: Removal of the fear of failure (Saturn), creates a happier, healthier, and more balanced condition (Venus), thus allowing one to prosper (Earth).

Uranus: Enjoying (Venus) fame through achievements in one's chosen field of endeavor (Earth) through invention or science (Uranus).

Neptune: Prosperity (Earth) through the helping of others (Neptune) along with the personal satisfaction it brings (Venus) into your life.

Pluto: Enjoying (Venus) fortune (Earth) from dealing with large groups (Pluto).

Planetary Hours: By applying the same definitions of the planetary influences, you can then select which hour of the day would be best for performing your magick.

The most common way of configuring the magickan's "day" is to begin counting the hours from sunrise and continuing on until sunrise the following day. Some use the midnight to midnight concept but that time sequence is scaled to a mundane world and is highly inaccurate for magickal purposes.

The first hour after sunrise is ruled by the planet the day represents. For example, the Sun rules the first hour of Sunday, The Moon rules the first hour of Monday, and so on throughout the week. The planet also rules the eighth, fifteenth, and twenty-second hours of that same day.

To clarify this, in our continuing use of the House of Taurus and the planet Venus as an example, your chosen day would be Friday because it, as well as Taurus, is ruled by the planet Venus. As stated previously, the first hour after sunrise on Friday is also ruled by the planet Venus, so this is the best time to create your talisman. You could also opt for the eighth, fifteenth, or twenty-second hour as well if you are not attuned to rising so early. This concept applies to all planets on the particular day that they rule.

Direction: Each element has a corresponding direction to face for the most favorable results when creating a talisman. They are as follows:

Earth: North   Air: East   Fire: South   Water: West

Elemental: In some forms of talisman construction, the energy or aid of an Elemental may be necessary. The enslavement of the elemental within the talisman is rarely done and then is only done for exceptional reasons. The story of Aladdin's Lamp is a good example of a talisman (the lamp) with an enslaved Elemental.

The elements, Earth, Air, Fire, and Water govern a specific direction as indicated previously. The individual elements also govern a specific type of an Elemental:

Earth: North: Gnomes and Trolls

Air: East: Sylphs

Fire: South: Salamanders

Water: West: Undines and Nymphs

Each of these separate groups has a distinct energy pattern and, when this energy is channeled into your talisman, the talisman becomes properly energized.

Symbol: Symbols have their own distinctive vibrational pattern; so, for this reason, each zodiac house has a symbol that vibrates uniquely to it.

Again referring to our example of the House of Taurus, symbolized by the Bull, and the planet Venus, the symbol of the Bull should be drawn or inscribed in some manner on copper or parchment on a Friday during the Planetary Hour of Venus. The inscribed copper or parchment would then be energized with the Elemental powers of Earth. The finished product would be a potent talisman for abundance.

Animals: In times long past, as well as in some Shamanic religions of the present day, Power Animals were used in magickal rites. They were painted on cave walls, on the human body, and on items of ritual significance. The Power Animals were summoned for their energy and influence, which was lent to humans. These powers could then be directed into people, objects, or places in order to create various types of changes, talismans, and power spots (Sacred places).

For those who are interested in utilizing the Power Animals, each zodiac house description offers suggestions as to what type of animal can be used most effectively with that house. As the type of animal varies greatly, these are only suggestions. When you call upon your Power Animal, it will tell you where it properly belongs by considering your background, what you are trying to achieve, and what will work best for you. Everyone's path will vary slightly so do not be alarmed if your neighbor has a Power Animal that comes to him or her from the North while the same animal might come to you from the East. Power Animals take into consideration your imbalances and bodily requirements, so, if you call upon energies that could harm or overload you, the Power Animal may come from the direction safest for you.

Once you are back in balance (assuming you had gotten out of balance), the Power Animal will again take up residency where its special energy is best presented.

Gems: The gems listed under each zodiac house serve a dual purpose. The first is for their folklore value in healing the most commonly found maladies within the house they reside in. Therefore, they can be used in talismans specifically designed for healing magick.

The second purpose of the gems listed is to assist you in the same manner as the Power Animals.

Fragrance/Scents: The various types of fragrances and scents listed are those most tuned to offer influence in the particular house under which they are found.

Parts of the Body: This section of associations will aid you in creating the proper talisman for healing and regulating different parts of the body. Use these associations in conjunction with the Power Animals, Gems, and Plants.

As disease is believed to begin from an imbalance in one's thinking, emotions, and aura, the listed animals, gems, fragrances, and plants will help adjust the imbalance and aid in the restoration of health.

A word of caution here is appropriate. Talisman magick and other forms of spiritual healing work from outside the body inward while the physical treatment of a competent health care professional is usually directed at the physical result of injury or disease.

We by no means infer that you should not seek the aid and treatment provided by a health care professional should you become injured or diseased. Use good judgment and caution in all your health care needs. The human body is both spiritual and physical so both must receive the proper care.

Plants: The various plants listed under this association are those mainly associated with healing and are excellent choices for inclusion in healing talismans. The remaining are in some way associated with magick that is attributed to a specific zodiac sign. These are best used as an offering or in the creation of a specific type of talisman indicated by the attributes of the house with which it is associated. And, just as with the power animals, you can channel the energy of a specific plant in order to em-power your work.

Gods and Goddesses: The Gods and Goddesses listed in no way comprise the entire listing of deities that have arisen throughout history. We have taken some of the most prominent names and listed them in specific ethnic and regional categories to help you find one that might fit your beliefs and background. The annotations accompanying each deity are brief but should give you an idea of each deity's function. The listings may also help you to understand the beliefs and histories of others by looking up the origins and specific functions of the various deities.

Besides being helpful in attaining a knowledge of the spiritual beliefs of others, the various deities may have more meaning to you than you might suspect. There are some, of other origins than yours, that might assist you into tapping into a past life. It is not at all unusual for an African American to find only a weak connection to the deities of Africa and a strong tie to a Celtic or Asian deity. The same might be said for a Chinese or Japanese person to be more at ease with a Native American deity. Remember, we are what we are in this incarnation only. Spiritual progression is not limited by race, religion, or gender.

As you progress along your chosen path in this life, you are encouraged to step beyond your physical ancestral roots. This is best done by exploring, with an open mind, as many of the various deities of history as possible. Select the ones with whom you have the most affinity for in-depth study. You will also find that, historically, the people who worshiped female deities and the people who worshiped male deities were quite different in their life styles. The male deity worshipers were, on the whole, more nomadic, and constantly waging war against one another (My God is tougher than your God).

In contrast, those who worshiped female deities were, in general, more passive, agriculturally oriented, and peace loving (all Goddesses are One). There are, of course, exceptions to everything but, in general, the descriptions are accurate.

The term "with an open mind" is very important here. An old saying about "One man's God is another man's Devil" is very true. A benevolent deity in one culture can seem to do a complete about face when that culture is taken over by another. The propaganda issued by the latter is usually negative in an attempt to sway the populace into worshiping the conquerer's deity.

History is full of "good" and "evil" deities. If you delve far enough into the history of the "evil" deity, you may find that the only reason that particular deity was branded as "evil" was that the deity was on the losing side in a war. Remember, most history books are written by the side who won the war.

Chapter 4 Quiz

1. Name the four basic Elements.
2. The Element of Earth governs the temper. T-F
3. The Moon governs Women's Mysteries. T-F
4. Water governs which direction?
5. The Elemental of Fire is the Salamander. T-F

Answers

1. Earth, Air, Water, and Fire.
2. False. Fire governs the temper; Earth governs all physical needs.
3. True.
4. West.
5. True.

PART THREE

History

5

A History of Talismans

One of the earliest non-verbal forms of communication known to be used by humans were symbolic replicas of familiar animals, insects, plants, and human figures adorned, at times, in animal skins. These crude facsimiles, whether painted upon the walls and ceilings of caves, or carved from bone, wood, stone, or horn, were our earliest amulets and talismans.

Some texts on the subject will refer to "amulets," "charms" and "talismans" in the same reference material, not bothering to differentiate, but there is a distinct difference between them. An amulet or charm is usually defined as an object, carried, worn, or hung on the body or dwelling wall, that is primarily for the protection of the wearer or those who dwell within. They are generally "natural" objects believed to ward off evil or to bring prosperity. That definition also fits a talisman, but the talisman has one more attribute that sets it apart. A talisman is an object, including an amulet or charm, that has been enlivened or consecrated with energy in order for it to perform a magickal function. It can be a natural object, or a specifically created combination of objects, scents, signs, colors, and metals, that is designed for a specific purpose, not limited to protection or prosperity. The task for which a talisman might be designed is limited only by the imagination and knowledge of the magickan.

The talisman is endowed with energy released from the human mind. The energies are channeled from universal or earthly origins, deities or angels, planets or elementals, or from one or more human minds concentrating during a ritual ceremony.

Based on archaeological interpretations, it can be inferred that the roots of symbolism, and its application to talismans, began during the pre-history of civilization when the first cave person felt the need to influence his environment through spiritual means.

Through scientific interpretation of archaeological findings, such as cave paintings, female figurines, and carved caricatures, the most common deduction is that the paintings and other items were more than just art but, in fact, had magickal and religious significance as well. The most common example of this are the numerous figurines, found throughout the world, of female configuration that represented "Mother Earth," or the "Mother Goddess."

Animals, plants, rocks, mountains, rivers and lakes, the sun, stars, and planets, almost everything the human eye could see, were believed to be alive and possess a spirit that often took the form of a deity.

The spirit was communicated with, through some form of ritual, to attain the co-operation of the deity housed within. Since it was normally unwise or inconvenient to meet an animal face to face, or to bring a mountain, tree, or river into the dwelling area, replicas were made in order to confront the spirit of the deity more conveniently and/or safely.

The religious leader, medicine man or woman, shaman or, by whatever name or title he or she might be called, usually performed a ritual designed to entice the spirit of the object into the effigy for communication purposes. Permission was then requested to kill it, in the case of an animal, for its flesh or other parts necessary for human survival, or a boon was asked from the spirit of the object believed capable of influencing the health, harvest, or security of the clan or tribe.

Many groups of humans, from prehistoric times down through the ages to the present American Indian tribes, named themselves collectively and individually after animals or objects believed to be influential or beneficial.

The attributes of animals, plants, or objects who were deified were assumed by individuals and tribes. Each individual or tribe had his or her or their own personal "totem" that protected the individual or tribe throughout life. (The "totem" could be classified as either an amulet or a talisman, depending on whether or not it was "charged.") Frequently, a part of a totem animal, such as a tooth, feather, or bone was worn on the body to keep the spirit of the animal close. These totems were called upon for wisdom, healing, or guidance.

So on down through the ages, from the cave people to the Sumerians, from the Babylonians to the Egyptians, the belief in amulets and talismans being divinely inspired has persisted. The creation epics of most religions are raft with examples of amulets and talismans. The Greater and Lesser Keys of Solomon are prime examples of talismans still popular today. They are found in almost every text dealing with talisman construction, so will not be covered by this book. There are numerous articles and manuscripts, some very well done, that go into great detail on the makeup of talismans. Migene Gonzalez-Wippler points out in her text entitled *The Complete Book of Amulets and Talismans*, 1991, that some of the instructions given on the consecration of talismans are somewhat exaggerated. She goes on to ask who would sacrifice an unblemished lamb to use its skin as virginal parchment?

In answer to her question, I doubt that anyone today would go that far because *it isn't necessary*. The zodiac talisman, described in this book, eliminates all the complicated, time consuming, and extravagant preparation associated with reproducing ancient talismans.

The procedures for making talismans, similar to those of King Solomon, can take months or years to complete. The intricate figures, the geometric designs, and the ritualistic procedures are difficult to learn and generally impossible to duplicate accurately without time consuming study and infinite patience. Our book, however, deals with the zodiac houses as the basis for simplified talismans, so we will stick with that.

For those of you who might be interested in Earth Magick or Shamanism and wish to construct an animal talisman, the following example will be extremely useful to you. In the example, we will choose a zodiac house that will help someone in a particular way. By placing the name or the image of the animal spirit helper into the chosen house, we will be calling upon it for help in the form of spiritual power.

In our example, let us assume that everyone has met, or knows of, someone who is defined as "meek as a mouse." That type of individual is usually one whom everyone seems to take advantage of. He or she is rarely heard to complain, nor does he or she ever seem to take any action to prevent this type of treatment.

Let us also assume that this meek individual really wants to step out of character and to become more assertive and aggressive. He or she is probably tired of being overlooked, underpaid, and taken for granted and would like to be popular and appreciated, but does not have the will power to carry it off.

Now, presume you are this person and you wish to select an animal helper to bring about the necessary change in your life. What type of animal would you choose? What zodiac house would you choose to place the animal in? How about a bear? Or a lion? No! Neither one of these would be exactly correct for the type of change we mentioned. While the bear or lion would impart aggressiveness, others would still cross swords with anyone displaying their traits.

How about a porcupine as an animal helper? Think about it for a minute. A porcupine goes most anywhere it wants to, does basically everything it wants to, and not too many animals will bother it. The temperament is assertive and the quills are sharp if rubbed the wrong way. It doesn't have to be loud or boisterous to get its way. People tend to fight those who are. A porcupine gets its way through respect of its tenacity and its playful and loving attitude. That is what is required here.

Next, you must decide which of the zodiac houses best represent the traits you are attempting to acquire. The House of Virgo, the house of the employer, would be satisfactory if you wish to enhance only the relationship with your boss and co-workers. The House of Capricorn could also be selected, as it is the house of occupational advancement.

By placing the porcupine into one or both of the houses, you are building a talisman using the signature (the unique vibration) of this animal. This means that you will take on the qualities this animal has to offer. You will become more loving and trusting and less "up tight." You will find more pleasure in your surroundings and in the people you work with. You will begin to feel your own power and establish a "territory" within your job.

Those who make the mistake of crossing you will wish they had not. You will be able to sharply, quickly, and quietly make your points, leaving no ground for argument or recourse. Thus is the power of the porcupine.

In the previous example, we could, just as easily, have used any one of the other nature categories as well. Perhaps a wasp would be chosen for a gorgeous figure, or a rose to increase romantic interests. In the case of a rose for romantic interests, be aware of the thorns. A rose without thorns is romantic, but is too vulnerable. A diamond is to be protected and valued, but not respected. What you choose depends on the outcome desired.

Be sure to read and re-read the attributes of each zodiac house. Understanding Key Words, Lessons, and Meanings is very important to your understanding the entire picture. The colors, days, metals, elements, planets, planetary hours, directions, elementals, symbols, animals, gems, scents, plants, and deities are all tied in to the Key Words, Lessons, and Meanings given. By mixing and matching the associations of various houses, based on the attributes of each, you can create the most detailed talisman possible; one that will be unique to your purpose. The possible choices of spiritual helpers are endless.

Chapter 5 Quiz

1. The act of "energizing" sets talismans apart from ordinary charms and amulets. T-F
2. Pre-history cave art has little significance other than childish art. T-F
3. The Greater and Lesser Keys of Solomon opened the royal executive washroom. T-F
4. Animal spirits can aid you in your life. T-F

5. Understanding the attributes of each zodiac house is unimportant to your comprehension of the entire magickal picture. T-F

Answers

1. True.
2. False. There is deep magickal and religious significance to prehistoric art.
3. False. They are talismans of ancient times still popular today.
4. True.
5. False. They are an essential segment in the total understanding of the concept of guiding your own destiny.

6

History of Symbols

As explained in the previous chapter, one of the earliest forms of non-verbal communication used by man was the pictogram or symbol. An inverted V indicating a mountain, a series of wavy lines representing water, or a human figure holding a spear with a bear nearby conveying that the man was hunting, are examples of the pictogram.

A pictogram is an image of something that can be observed or felt. A symbol, as defined in *Webster's New Universal Unabridged Dictionary*, is "a sign by which one infers a thing . . ." and "something that stands for or represents another thing." A pictogram (*petrogram* if painted on rock and *petroglyph* if carved in rock) is a simple symbol or series of symbols, drawings, imprints, replicas, or gestures that will communicate a message. They generally transcend language barriers, most symbols being universal in design. If you were to visit a foreign land and knew nothing of its language, you would still be able to communicate through symbolic hand gestures and drawings.

Symbols can be as simple as a drawing of an arrow showing direction or as complicated as the script of an alphabet. As you read the words written on this page, we are communicating with you by symbols. You may not understand all the symbols if they are written in a language other than your own, because the symbols used here are not universal. They are the written script symbols of the English language.

Let us now take a look, for example, at the English word BEAR. Suppose instead of the script symbols B E A R, I had used a symbol that looked like a drawing of a bear. Then no

81

matter what language you spoke or understood, you would know what I meant. This is undoubtedly how early humans communicated before spoken language was discovered. Org would show Morg a drawing of a bear while holding up his spear. Morg would then know that Org was going bear hunting.

From the time that Org first drew the pictograph or symbol of the bear, to the modern day version of Org driving his automobile through rush hour traffic, our lives have been immersed in symbols.

The ancient Assyrian-Babylonian symbolic writing known as cuneiform was an offshoot of an even earlier form of symbolic writing developed by the Sumerians thousands of years prior. These wedge-shaped pictographs have been deciphered because archaeologists understood the language of symbols. By studying the history of man's writings and drawings, the past comes alive far easier than it does by studying old bones and flint knives.

The next step up from the pictogram for man was the development of the ideogram. The conversion of the pictogram to the ideogram required a bit more imagination and intelligence on the part of the reader as well as an agreement within the society or tribe to accept the additional meanings.

The ideogram adds some general concept or attribute to the simple pictogram. For example, a poster with a picture of a cigarette on it merely indicates or suggests a cigarette; but when a circle is inscribed about it and an X character is superimposed over the cigarette within the circle, we get the idea that "No Smoking" is allowed.

According to Professor Mario Pei (*What's in a Word?* 1968), ideograms played important roles in Egyptian hieroglyphics. The hieroglyphic pictogram showing an old, bent-over man leaning on a staff originally, as a pictogram, meant nothing more than "old man," but eventually it came to mean "aging," "decrepit" or "to lean upon" as an ideogram.

The magickan who wishes to construct the most potent talismans possible must also understand the language of symbols. Symbolic configurations inscribed upon a talisman enhance the power many times.

In order to understand the language of symbols, we must continue to explore their origins. As stated above, early man used symbols that represented various animals, plants, and geographic sites to communicate. He also needed a way to communicate with his deities. He undoubtedly felt that a symbolic representation of the deity would suffice. But as man grew in knowledge and his religious beliefs became more sophisticated, he needed some way to contact the deities by a more spiritual means. He needed magickal symbols.

Again according to Professor Mario Pei (1968), people became busier and needed to find some simple way of conveying a complicated concept. Rather than draw the figure of a man or woman, a scribe devised a symbol to indicate a human being. The concept evolved into a very useful shorthand step in the evolution of written communication.

There are two general types of symbols. The natural symbol and the artificial symbol. The natural symbols are mainly derived by suggestions or inferences implied when a natural object is viewed. A mountain, for example, is a natural symbol. It suggests strength, majesty and power.

The artificial symbol, on the other hand, is created to represent beliefs, perceptions, and concepts formed in the human mind. Examples of these might be the construction symbols found on a blueprint of a building. To the layman they might be indecipherable, but to the trained engineer they are as familiar a means of communication as normal language.

The symbolic language of the magickan is a combination of natural and artificial signs (mystical symbols) that have been developed over time by intelligent men and women.

How was this done? According to the Rosicrucians, these same men and women studied and observed nature to learn the true ways of her operations. They also looked toward the heavens above and down at the earth below.

They found that when certain things happen, again and again, certain conditions prevail. Man discovered that phenomena depend on basic, uniform conditions. These uniform conditions of dependency are the Laws; irrevocable Cosmic Truths.

These natural laws formed symbols within men's minds that defined events. They realized that the meaning perceived in a law of nature created in the mind its own symbol.

There are many examples of true mystical symbols. The All Seeing Eye, the star or pentacle, the triangle, the circle and other geometrically perfect designs, the cross, the runic inscriptions, the trigrams and hexagrams of the I Ching, and the signs of the zodiac are but a few.

Therefore, there are no substitutes for true mystical symbols. A mystical symbol is the very thought form of the Cosmic Law itself. Languages, customs and governments change, but ancient designs of mystical symbols remain forever intact because they are based on incorruptible laws of the universe.

Chapter 6 Quiz

1. One of the earliest forms of non-verbal communication used by man was the ideogram. T-F
2. What is the difference between a pictogram, a petrogram, and a petroglyph?
3. Cuneiform is a form of writing using wedge shaped pictograms. T-F
4. There are substitutes for true mystical symbols. T-F
5. The ideogram adds what to a pictogram?

Answers

1. False. The pictogram.
2. A petrogram is a pictogram painted on rock while a petroglyph is a pictogram carved in rock.
3. True.
4. False.
5. A general concept or attitude that is widely accepted by society.

7

History of Numerology and Alphabets

The ancient Chaldeans, Egyptians, Greek, Romans, and Chinese, and other advanced civilizations of the Arabs, Africans, Hebrews, and Japanese, understood that numerology was the study of the vibration of numbers. Numbers were studied by every civilized people as an intricate part of their mathematics, religion, magick, and science.

Some of the oldest talismans in recorded history have been either based on numbers or have been numbers themselves. It is therefore logical that their use should play an important role in the zodiac talisman.

Pythagoras summed up numerology by stating, "Everything is disposed according to the numbers." He believed all things to be numbers, and the elements of numbers are the elements of all things.

From this summation, we can state that each number represents a frequency of vibration, just as everything in the universe vibrates to its own unique frequency.

Numbers are thought to be the most primitive element of order in the human mind and are used by the subconscious as an ordering factor (Jung). Our thoughts are communicated through the use of languages that are based on numerical symbolism. Thus the alpha characters and numbers are intricately interwoven.

For centuries, people have believed that names carry power or denote the characteristics of an individual. Frequently, ancient

85

peoples would give their children two names. One was for the
immediate family and one was for the clan, tribe, or society in
which he or she lived. There was often a third name bestowed
when the child became an adult or became a practitioner of
magick.

This third name was a closely guarded secret, as it was believed that to know the "true" name of an individual was to
have power over him. This seems to have been an almost universal belief in every culture and every system of magick known
to man.

As an example, the Gnostics, believing this to be true, spent a
great deal of time attempting to discover the many ancient and
secret names of "God" through numerology. To them, success
would have meant power over that deity for whatever purpose
they chose.

For the Gnostics, this idea came about because the Phoeni-
cians, in the second millennium B.C., were the first to discover
the principle of alphabetic writing. The Greeks learned it from
them and they spread it to the rest of the world.

The next phase entailed the idea of writing numbers by means
of letters. The Greeks, Arabs, Jews, and Syrians each began
doing this by assigning a numerical value to each letter of their
respective alphabets, thus giving each word or combination of
letters a total numerical value. This became the basis of the
mystical religious doctrine called *Gematria* by the Cabalists and
Isopsephia by the Greeks and Gnostics. As mentioned earlier, the
Gnostics used this method to find the true names of God.

This same procedure was followed by the Cabalist, Christian,
and Moslem esoterists when making symbolic interpretations
and calculations for predicting the future. It also is the basis of
dream interpretations and talisman construction.

It can then be surmised that whether one chooses to use
numbers or alpha characters for creating a talisman, the results
will be the same. A particular number has an equivalent alpha
character, thus both have the same variation and root meaning.

These vibrations draw that which they represent. By choosing
a specific number or letter, you are consciously creating new
energy in your life. This is another way of making a talisman.
You can actually make drastic changes in your life by changing
your name, changing the spelling of your existing name, or by

choosing an address or automobile license plate that vibrates correctly for you.

Below is an example of number and letter relationships similar to that used by the ancient Hebrews.

1	2	3	4	5	6	7	8	9
A	B	C	D	E	F	G	H	I

10	20	30	40	50	60	70	80	90
J	K	L	M	N	O	P	Q	R

100	200	300	400	500	600	700	800	
S	T	U	V	W	X	Y	Z	

In our example, the number 45 could be written as "ME." God could be written as $7 + 60 + 4 = 71$.

THE PYTHAGOREAN METHOD (EXOTERIC)

This method is the most popular in the western world and reveals only that which is obvious, not what is hidden.

1	2	3	4	5	6	7	8	9
A	B	C	D	E	F	G	H	I
J	K	L	M	N	O	P	Q	R
S	T	U	V	W	X	Y	Z	

ALPHABET AND NUMERICAL EQUIVALENTS

Zero or 0:	Incubation, forming, not yet manifest.
A, J, S, 1:	New soul, birth, rebirth, beginnings.
B, K, T, 2:	Balance, marriage, union, puberty.
C, L, U, 3:	Product, children, reward from labor.
D, M, V, 4:	Foundation, stability, rut, boredom.
E, N, W, 5:	Changing, moving, growing, fluid.
F, O, X, 6:	Supervisor, family, laborers.
G, P, Y, 7:	Spirituality, understanding.
H, Q, Z, 8:	Success, the businessman.
I, R, 9:	Humanitarian, reformer, sage.

THE CHALDEAN METHOD (ESOTERIC)

The Chaldean method of numerology is considered more accurate than the Pythagorean as it reveals that which is hidden, a more occult or metaphysical vein to the destiny within a person's character.

This method was developed by the Chaldeans who occupied southern Babylonia many centuries ago. Lloyd Strayhorn, in his book *Numbers and You*, 1980/7, states that ". . . the people of Chaldea became well known for their contributions to astronomy, mathematics, and other sciences, particularly astrology and numerology. So adept were these Chaldean people in the metaphysical arts, that their name became synonymous with such studies."

Mr. Strayhorn also states, "All numbers, whether found under this or the Pythagorean one, have basically the same meanings, symbols, nature and caricature."

1	2	3	4	5	6	7	8
A	B	C	D	E	U	O	F
I	K	G	M	H	V	Z	P
J	R	L	T	N	W		
Q		S		X			
Y							

In the Chaldean method, the numbers run from 1 through 8. The number 9 was considered a sacred or holy number and therefore was not used.

To use either the Pythagorean or the Chaldean method, write out a name and birth date as follows:

Birth date: May (month)   02 (day)   1955 (year)
                    5+   2+   20 = 27 = 9

Next, refer to the birth number in this example. The number 9 indicates destiny under the Pythagorean system, while the day of birth, 2, represents the personality and other factors under the Chaldean system.

Pythagorean: K   A   L   A
$$2 + 1 + 3 + 1 = 7$$

P   A   J   E   O   N
$$7 + 1 + 1 + 5 + 6 + 5 = 25 = 7$$
$$7 + 7 = 14 = 5$$
Birth number = 9   Name number = 5

The world views Kala Pajeon as a number 5, a changing, growing individual. The individual names both factor to a 7, spirituality and understanding. The birth number 9 reveals her destiny as a humanitarian, reformer, and sage. Remember, the Pythagorean method is an exoteric method, a view of the external person or how you would view Kala if you met her.

Chaldean: K   A   L   A
$$2 + 1 + 3 + 1 = 7$$

P   A   J   E   O   N
$$8 + 1 + 1 + 5 + 7 + 5 = 27 = 9$$
$$7 + 9 = 16 = 7$$
Birth Day number = 2   Name number = 7

Under the Chaldean system, we see the inner or esoteric Kala. The first name factors to a 7, spirituality and understanding. The last name factors to a 9, humanitarian, reformer, and sage. The combined number of the first and last name is 7. The birth number 2 reveals a balanced union within life.

By viewing a person, in this case Kala Pajeon, through both exoteric (Pythagorean) and esoteric (Chaldean) numerological systems, we can tell whether the inner person is the same as that person the world views. In our example, Kala is revealed to be the same person within as the world views without.

As there are so many numerological systems in the world, we have compiled a general meaning for each of the numbers from 0 to 9 by choosing the most common associations given to each number by the majority of the systems. They are as follows:

0: Incubation, unmanifested, forming, year.
1: New beginnings, birth, starting, a gain.

2: Balance, harmony, unions, partnerships.
3: Producing, offspring, creation, product.
4: Solid foundation.
5: Quick change or alteration.
6: Home, work, family, stability and management.
7: Spirituality.
8: Success.
9: Ending.

Double numbers: By integrating the attributes of each of the single numbers, a combined meaning is generated. For example, combining the aspects of 1 and 0 creates great power. Something wild and powerful is manifesting here.

Another example might be the numbers 3 and 4. Here we would be creating or producing a solid basis for a particular action.

In summation, the idea of this chapter was not to teach numerology or the total history of alphabets. Our main purpose was to inform you that numbers and letters vibrate to significant meanings. As talismans, numbers and letters are very influential.

When you make your talisman using our Zodiac Worksheet, it is important to write in the center circle all information you possess about a person, place, or thing you are attempting to influence. Examples of this information are dates of birth, telephone numbers, street addresses, social security numbers, military I.D. numbers, drivers license numbers, and anything else that you can think of.

It is not necessary to break down this information into numerological patterns on the worksheet. It is enough that you write them in properly and correctly. They will then act as a whole when influencing the outcome.

Chapter 7 Quiz

1. The quote "Everything is disposed according to the numbers" is attributed to whom?
2. Knowing an individual's "True name" is to have power over him. T-F

3. Either numbers or alpha characters can be used in talisman construction with the same results. T-F
4. The Chaldeans did not use the number 9 in their method of numerology. Why?
5. The Pythagorean Method of Numerology is esoteric or exoteric?

Answers

1. Pythagoras.
2. True, according to numerologists and occultists.
3. True.
4. The number 9 was considered a sacred or holy number and therefore was not used.
5. Exoteric.

PART FOUR

Divination Systems

8

The I Ching

A BRIEF HISTORY OF THE I CHING

The I Ching is believed to have been discovered circa 3000 B.C.E. by Fu Hsi, a legendary Emperor and hero of China.

Sometime in the legendary past of ancient China, Fu Hsi was strolling on the banks of the Hwang Ho River, when a mythical creature appeared before him in the water. This creature, called a hippogriff, was said to have been half horse and half griffin. As it rose from the water, blocking the Emperor's path, the creature turned its back to the Emperor and exposed eight trigrams inscribed on its hind quarters.

Exactly how Emperor Fu Hsi discovered the initial eight trigrams is lost to history and may never be truthfully discovered. He is credited with naming the trigrams and ascribing their attributes and images. The important thing here, however, is that he observed that they represented the fact that all things undergo change, hence the name "I Ching" or "The Book of Changes."

Change is the basic foundation of all Heavenly and Earthly affairs. It is beyond the control of man but it can be influenced. With the I Ching, when one's future is predicted, choices are offered. The future depends on what action is taken regarding a predicted situation.

Many scholars believe that it was King Wen (1171 to 1122 B.C.E.), the credited founder and father to the Chou dynasty (approximately 1111 to 249 B.C.E.), who expounded upon the original eight trigrams and created the sixty-four Hexagrams.

Still others believe it was the Duke of Chou, King Wen's son, who developed the sixty-four Hexagrams from his father's notes. It was from these notes that the "Chou I," or "The Changes of Chou," developed into a full dissertation. One could now discover not only what problems lay in the immediate future, but what course of action was best taken to solve the problems.

The Ten Wings, attributed to Confucius, contain the oldest commentary literature relating to the I Ching. Although this authorship has been disputed, it is recognized that Confucius was a scholar of the I Ching in his later years.

In more modern times, the respected psychiatrist Carl Jung utilized the I Ching and was amazed by its accuracy. With such noted scholars and professionals impressed by the I Ching, it is no wonder that it is widely used today.

However, as with most esoteric symbols that hide the secret wisdom of a civilization, the I Ching has been used primarily for divination. Unfortunately, this alone does not do justice to the wisdom, nor the philosophy, it has to offer.

As previously stated, any symbols, particularly those that have been used for long periods of time, take on the energies or vibrations of the meanings attributed to them. For that reason alone, the I Ching can be used effectively as a talisman, since each symbol represents a specific concept or idea that has been manifested for thousands of years by millions of meditators. This makes them a very powerful tool.

THE I CHING

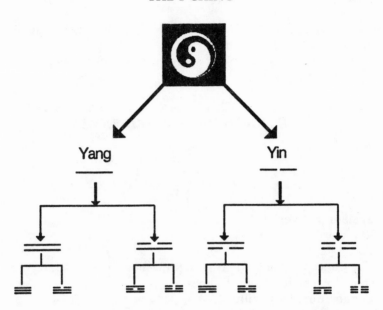

The Chinese I Ching are a series of sixty-four hexagrams. The basis of the Chinese I Ching is in the theory that everything is composed of either female or male energy and various combinations thereof.

It is a system of harmony and balance as denoted by the symbols of yin and yang. Therefore, the terms negative and positive do not denote that one is better or lesser that the other, but is in fact a set of exact opposites and as such attract one another to create a perfect and complete whole. One without the other creates imbalance and, only then, begets harm within one's life, body, or thoughts.

YAO BAR

The hexagrams of the I-Ching are formed from solid and broken lines called "Yao Bars" or "Line Bars." The line representing the "Yin" or "female energy" is broken in the center, while the line representing the "Yang" or "male energy" is solid.

Yin or Female Energy: Dark, inactive and silent. Its polarity is electromagnetically negative (−).

Yang or Male Energy: Bright and active. Its polarity is electro-magnetically positive (+).

THE EIGHT ORIGINAL TRIGRAMS

Ch'ien

Symbol: Heaven
Key word: Creative
Color: Red
Key Concepts: Yang, great strength, action, reason; strong creative power, durability, firmness
Connotation: Perpetuity
Associated People: Rulers
Element: Metal (Earth)

Tui
Yang

Symbol: Lake
Key Word: Ecstasy
Color: White
Key Concepts: Yang, joy, bliss, sensuality, tenderness, satisfaction
Connotation: Incomplete
Associated People: Young Females
Element: Water

Li

Symbol: Sun
Key Word: Enlightenment
Color: Purple
Key Concepts: Yang, clinging, tenacity, brightness, beauty, elegance, intelligence
Connotation: Perception
Associated People: Midlife females.
Element: Fire

Chen

Symbol: Thunder
Key Word: Action (based on inspiration)
Color: Yellow
Key Concepts: Yang, energy, violence, awakening, trembling, execution, extending
Connotation: Arousing
Associated People: Famous, royalty
Element: Wood (Earth)

Sun

Symbol: Wind
Key Word: Penetration (through greatness)
Color: Green
Key Concepts: Yin, justice, gentleness, dissolution, progress, toughness
Connotation: Remoteness
Associated People: Older females, business persons
Element: Wood (Earth)

K'an

Symbol: Water
Key Word: Caution
Color: Deep Red
Key Concepts: Yin, instinctivity, fearlessness, defilement, difficulty
Connotation: Danger
Associated People: Midlife males
Element: Water

Ken

Symbol: Mountain
Key Word: Stillness
Color: Yellow
Key Concepts: Yin, meditation, withdrawal, peace, tranquility
Connotation: Serenity
Associated People: Young males.
Element: Earth

Kun

Symbol: Earth
Key Word: Receptive
Color: Black
Key Concepts: Yin, fertility, fulfillment, passivity, dedication, patience
Connotation: Without rest
Associated People: The average person
Element: Earth

* * *

Trigrams are properly read from the bottom to the top, or starting inward and working outward as demonstrated in the diagram.

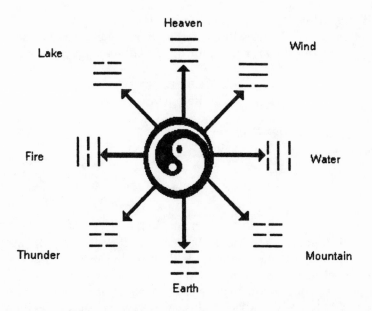

From the basic eight trigrams came sixty-four hexagrams, derived by placing one trigram atop another. The bottom (since the trigram is properly read from the bottom up) is considered dominant and generally has more influence.

THE 64 HEXAGRAMS OF THE I-CHING

1. CH'EIN: Heaven
The Creative

Heaven Over Heaven

The Universal and Creative processes are at their peak of power and potency. Power is unlimited and success is assured. None can oppose the person who uses this hexagram in magick. This is the hexagram of the Sage.

Waxing Moon: To build strength and power.
Waning Moon: To tear down seemingly impenetrable defenses, lies, or fabrications. Perfect for unjust lawsuits against you.

2. K'UN: Earth
The Receptive

Earth Over Earth

This hexagram represents the energy and power of Earth and all the magick She contains. It governs the manifestation of material needs, wisdom, and the power to succeed.

When using K'un, material success is assured, but be prepared to follow the advice of those wiser and possibly older than yourself. This may include contacting the magickal kingdoms (elementals) for guidance as well.

The secret of K'un's power lies within its ability to adapt, learn, mold, and bend to the needs of any circumstance. This is the reason it will succeed where all others fail. Patience, cunning, cleverness, and the wisdom of knowing when to act and when to be still are the gifts of K'un.

Waxing Moon: To build material success and enhance wisdom.
Waning Moon: To dissipate baleful magick, power corruption, or monetary empires.

3. CHUN: Sprouting
Difficulty at the Beginning

Water Over Thunder

This hexagram denotes new beginnings; the birthing process. Unfortunately, as with anything upon the threshold of manifestation, it is vulnerable and unstable. Thus, its growing pangs are seen as obstacles.

Waxing Moon: To build or manifest something new; ideas, situations, and relations.

Waning Moon: To tear down old and stagnant situations that no longer serve one's highest good and allow for rebirth.

4. MENG: Folly and Youthful Rebellion
Inexperience

```
━━━━━━━━
━━  ━━
━━  ━━
━━  ━━
━━━━━━━━
━━  ━━
```

Mountain Over Water

This hexagram suggests that something has been born or has manifested. However, as with anything that is immature, it is vulnerable until certain lessons have been learned and created a strong maturity. Inexperience may lead to childish folly and for that reason caution should be used and wise advice sought.

Use this hexagram to represent anyone (or a situation) with an innocent or childish nature; someone ruled by emotions and need rather than logic and common sense.

Waxing Moon: Surround this hexagram with others that are strong, wise and protective. If you are protecting a child, place the hexagram in Leo.

Waning Moon: When using this hexagram on a waning moon, it helps to rid the person or situation of the elements that create immaturity.

5. HSU: Waiting
Calculated Waiting

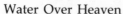

Water Over Heaven

Waiting is for the wise, and this hexagram promises victory over the darkness of the unknown and the dangers therein. The key to success here is in simply exercising patience, reserving strength, and using common sense.

Just as a cat does not spring into action before the mouse has left the hole, success is not achieved through brash action.

This is an excellent hexagram for lawyers and shrewd business professionals.

Waxing Moon: To build ultimate victory by watching and waiting for the right time to act.

Waning Moon: To persuade others to make a foolish move in your favor or to your benefit.

6. SUNG: Conflict
Lawsuits and Disagreements are Resolved

Heaven Over Water

There have been disagreements, but whether you are innocent or guilty, to persevere you must be prepared to wait and negotiate to reach an equitable solution. Be prepared to compromise and bend if necessary; this can only be to your benefit.

Sung also represents civil action, and is closely associated with the 7th zodiac House of Libra.

Patience and an unbiased evaluation of the entire situation, including the part you may have played in bringing it about, will assure your success.

Waxing Moon: To bring any dispute to an end. When placed in the 7th zodiac House of Libra you can build your defense and success.

Waning Moon: To postpone or avoid the settling of a dispute until a more advantageous time is found.

When placed in the 7th zodiac House of Libra on a waning moon, you can break down or reveal the flaws of other's testimony or claim of innocence.

7. SHIH: Army
Collective Force through Organized Leadership

Earth Over Water

This is a curious hexagram with intense and fascinating meanings. On the one hand it deals with large groups of people and their energy. It also imparts great wisdom, victory, strength, and leadership abilities.

On a deeper level, it suggests that the capability for greatness and power comes from within. It is this ability to control one's own energy that will determine the success or failure in any project or situation.

Waxing Moon: To create power, control, success, and prestige for controlling groups.

Waning Moon: Used to break up groups or corrupt regimes of any kind.

8. PI: To Hold Together and Unite
To Unite Under Wise Leadership

Water Over Earth

Great leaders must be well organized and clear thinking, while remaining unbiased toward all. To dole out discipline fairly and equally, one must learn to bend and compromise when attempting to unite unruly factions. Strength, clear thinking, and strategy bring success.

Waxing Moon: Use this hexagram to unite groups or factions that cannot agree while under your leadership.

Waning Moon: To breakup or expose corrupt leadership.

9. HSIAO CH'U: Limit or Tame
The Weak Temporarily Conquer the Strong

Wind Over Heaven

Anyone in need of help or support from those in power would find this a useful hexagram.

The hexagram represents the power of the weak or small (insignificant) to tame, limit, persuade, manipulate, or temporarily control those in a position of power. However, you must act quickly as the influence of this hexagram is of short duration only.

Waxing Moon: To build power, strength, and control over those in a position of power. Ideal for business, government, politics, and court cases.

Waning Moon: Use to tear down the resistance of those in a position of power.

10. LU: Treading or Conduct
The Weak, No Obvious Threat When Treading with Respect

Heaven Over Lake

To gain or maintain power by exhibiting controlled calm, good nature, and feigned innocence. This happy-go-lucky and non-threatening appearance wins you favor. It allows you to ultimately mold and control any situation without threatening and alarming those in power.

Waxing Moon: The use of this hexagram can make one appear harmless, but there is power and purpose hidden behind the calm and smiling face. Equate this hexagram to the Greeks and their Trojan Horse.

Waning Moon: Use this hexagram when a situation, person, or company is not as it appears or promises.

11. T'AI: Peace and Prosperity
Harmony, Peace, Goodness, Happiness, and Success

Earth Over Heaven

This is a strong hexagram representing abundance and success in all endeavors. Peace, harmony, productivity, and goodwill; the powerful share their prosperity with those less fortunate.

Waxing Moon: To build prosperity and advance within the ranks of the powerful. A very good hexagram for business, politics, and family life.

Waning Moon: To tear down, break up, or weaken a prosperous and harmonious situation or atmosphere. Using T'ai on the waning moon creates (#12) P'I, stagnation, turmoil, and disharmony.

12. P'I: Stagnation or Standstill
A Blocked Condition

Heaven Over Earth

This hexagram depicts confusion, stagnation, and a totally blocked condition or situation. With this hexagram, you can expect back stabbings, humiliations, lies, deceit, slander, gossip, bad advice, and deliberate attempts to make someone or something fail.

Waxing Moon: Manifests total chaos and strengthens enemies. The good, innocent, or virtuous cannot win against the corrupt.

Waning Moon: To break up the chaos and create (#11) T'ai, a balanced, harmonious and victorious condition for the just.

13. T'UNG JEN: Fellowship with Men or Community
A Small Group Led by One and Acting As One

Heaven Over Fire

Good friends, acquaintances, and fellowship; prosperity comes with the use of this hexagram. There is wisdom and strength in numbers. Help comes from good advisors, colleagues, and teachers.

There is one key figure that is the nucleus of these good relations. He or she is a wise person, willing to bend, and mediate and harmonize strongly within the group by subtle intervention.

Waxing Moon: To encourage and promote sound relationships with others; to be united as one and gain prosperity for all. Use this hexagram when trying to win the friendship, love, or admiration of others. It is perfect for use in any open or closed negotiations. Use to become the nucleus of leadership.

Waning Moon: Some groups work and conspire to harm others and, for that reason, it is best that they destroy themselves from within. The T'ung Jen hexagram would undermine the harmony and create disputes.

14. TA YU: Possessions in Great Measure
Sovereignty, Community, and Wise Leadership Success

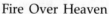

Fire Over Heaven

This is an excellent hexagram for working with large groups of people with varying needs where communication and a common ground must be found in order to obtain success for all.

Waxing Moon: When starting new projects this hexagram helps you to find a common ground for understanding the needs of those who support you. It will help to strengthen the inner character and support harmonious relations between yourself and others.

Waning Moon: To dissipate communal spirit, support, and cooperation in any community or political endeavor.

15. CH'IEN: Modesty
Humility, Moderation, and Inner Contemplation Success

Earth Over Mountain

This is an interesting hexagram that speaks of great success through moderation, modesty, or humility in spirit, and wise council and service to others.

It is often used for public servants or elected officials. It speaks of honesty in one's position, which brings honor, where deceit brings dishonor.

It warns against all extremes, as this hexagram works toward moderation in all things. Moderation brings balance, peace, and harmony into one's life.

Waxing Moon: To build positive public relations and assist in listening more and speaking less. Knowing when to speak, the proper things to say, and to whom to say them are within the scope of this hexagram.

Waning Moon: This hexagram on the waning moon clouds the mind from truth, honor, and humility. It emphasizes ineptness and publicly discredits.

16. YU: Enthusiasm
Loyalty and Devotion of Others to You

Thunder Over Earth

To change the course of events and gain the support of others, Yu is an excellent start. But do not get carried away, this is only the beginning of change and your supporters are still few, but growing. Therefore, proceed slowly, conserve energy and you will succeed.

Waxing Moon: To create a change in accordance to your will and wishes.

Waning Moon: To tear down the existing situation so that something new (that you will specify on the waxing moon) can manifest.

17. SUI: Following, Adapting, or Harmonizing
Learning to Re-adapt to Nature Brings Great Success

Lake Over Thunder

By following Mother Nature (wisdom) and Her laws (magick), great success is achieved. But if one follows the teachings of the Mother without pleasure or joy, no benefit will be gained.

This hexagram also represents the allure a young woman can have upon an older man and the usurping of power by the weak from the strong.

Waxing Moon: If you wish to lock a secret away, this is the hexagram to use.

If you are a young person and wish to win the heart or favor of an older man or woman, use Sui.

Waning Moon: To learn magick and any other secret, whether past, present, or future, simply place this hexagram in the house where you believe there is a secret to be had and watch that secret unfold before you.

Use to expose a young person that is using wiles to capture the heart of an older and much wealthier man or woman.

18. KU: To Replace or Repair Natural Decay
To Repair and Replace Rot in Advance Brings Success

Mountain Over Wind

In all things, it is the natural course of events to have decay. This requires, from time to time, reassessment, repair, and improvement upon the original. Without this repair, decay turns to chaos and total destruction, but periodic reassessments, adjustments, and repair maintain growth and progress.

Waxing Moon: Whenever a person, situation or relationship needs repair and improvement, this is the hexagram to use.

Waning Moon: There are times when a situation or relationship may not warrant repairs. In such a case, Ku can be used to help make the final break.

19. LIN: Approaching Greatness
A Time of Great Power Approaches

Earth Over Lake

Power through inspiring, motivating, and leading others gives one the title of being a great leader. This hexagram brings great fame, fortune, and happiness.

As Lin denotes the absolute peak of power and happiness, it is wise to realize this perfection will be fleeting. Take advantage of this time and be prepared to move quickly on.

Waxing Moon: Use this hexagram when you need a quick victory and are prepared to progress swiftly.

Waning Moon: When you need to attack a powerful opponent or enemy, Lin will give you a moment to strike, but be prepared for your opponent's eventual recovery and backlash.

20. KUAN: Contemplation
View Problems and Seek Inner Knowing for Solutions

Wind Over Earth

Use this hexagram when you need to wisely and closely analyze a situation that will ultimately affect others. This is particularly true when the decision affects commerce, and others' physical well being (as in business, law, politics).

Waxing Moon: To build wisdom and inner contemplation for a successful and competent decision.

Waning Moon: Kuan used on the waning moon can block the competent decisions of another. It can also be used to dismantle antiquated laws or political decisions.

21. SHI HO: Biting Through
Right Wrongs, Create Reforms, and Carry-Out Justice

Fire over Thunder

This hexagram symbolizes the dispensing of justice and acting upon necessary measures of reform. Such action can be tedious and sometimes unpleasant, but without such action, new growth or progress cannot be made.

It also represents criminal actions brought to justice and, for that reason, has an affinity to the 7th Zodiac House of Libra, which rules, judges, and dispenses sentences upon criminal action.

In effect, Shi Ho is used to clear the way or path of anything blocking progress, be it people, crimes, or situations.

Waxing Moon: To build your case of innocence and offer protection against false judgments.

Waning Moon: Used on the waning moon, it would tear down or allow others to clearly see the weaknesses within the defending or accusing party's case.

22. PI: Grace or Beauty
Beauty Is Illusory

Mountain Over Fire

Pi is a curious hexagram as it essentially states that "Beauty is only skin deep." Pi attracts the attention of many who are drawn to its radiant beauty. However, exterior or surface conditions seldom give a fair appraisal of what lies hidden beneath that lovely surface.

Consider Pi as a way to open doors. Once in, you will need to prove yourself worthy to keep the position you have so easily won with your appearance.

Pi also refers to a state of grace, in which all within you is now balanced and bringing forth new opportunities and happiness.

Waxing Moon: Used on a waxing moon, it will attract many lovers; in business, it will draw people as if you were a magnet. Use Pi to create an inner state of harmony, beauty, and balance; with this use comes great magickal power.

Waning Moon: To repel others, opportunities and create inner disharmony.

23. PO: Splitting or Breaking Apart
Deterioration, Destruction and Chaos

```
━━━━━━━
━━  ━━
━━  ━━
━━  ━━
━━  ━━
━━  ━━
```

Mountain Over Earth

Po speaks of things that have been allowed to rot away until they break apart. It is a time of total chaos and disorder, but from this decay will come rebirth, for all things work in cycles. Before there can be a re-birth, something must give way to death.

Waxing Moon: When something has outlived its usefulness, it must be set aside for something new and better; although this seldom seems to happen as a general rule. For that reason, Po, used on a waxing moon, will make it clear that change is imminent, with or without the support of others.

Waning Moon: If the changes are coming too fast and uncontrolled, slow them down or stop them altogether.

24. FU: To Return
Return to the Point of Error for a New Direction

Earth Over Thunder

Fu is excellent when you need to correct any error, fault, situation, or action. It opens new doors and new directions, giving one a second chance.

Waxing Moon: When an error has been made in life, use Fu for new opportunities to correct the wrong.

Waning Moon: Use when a wrong has been committed and it needs to be made known or uncovered; also to diminish the effects of a great wrong, thus allowing one to build (upon the following waxing moon) new opportunities to correct the mistake.

25. WU WANG: Innocence
Innocence is No Excuse. Expect the Unexpected

Heaven Over Thunder

There are times when being innocent (in heart, mind, thought, and soul) in a certain situation is not enough. The unexpected strikes and spoils all good and sincere efforts.

Even the most innocent actions and good intentions can lead one into serious trouble and mistakes; and, can sometimes make one a victim of an otherwise avoidable situation.

Being forewarned and thus arming one's self with knowledge and inner awareness will avoid these types of problems. Watch your thoughts and your own intentions for guile.

Waxing Moon: Use Wu Wang to draw magickal protection around you from the energies of Mother Earth. This protects you from those that would cause you harm, and avoids mistakes or accidents.

Waning Moon: To push away those influences that would cause harm or mishap.

26. TA CH'U: Taming Power of the Great
Restraint Accumulates Wealth and Power for Action

Mountain Over Heaven

To store potential energy takes wise restraint. Once this energy has been sufficiently stored, it can be used when the time is right to create great abundance.

Waxing Moon: Build your energy with Ta Ch'u on the waxing moon. If you feel you cannot house this energy within yourself, store the energy within an object or symbol.

For example, create the symbol of Ta Ch'u in Jade (the color should be harmonious with your purpose) and then palm the Jade. Pour all your excess energy into the stone. Do this over a period of time and whenever your energy is low; just holding or thinking of the stone will energize you. Over a period of years the stone becomes an extremely powerful talisman.

Waning Moon: Extreme caution must be used when creating a Ta Ch'u talisman on the waning moon. Research your stones carefully, choose one that absorbs, but cannot release. Such a stone would be black Tourmaline. Where the Jade is given energy and stores it for future use, the Tourmaline can be made to steal energy from anyone it contacts.

The Tourmaline stores this energy which can be accessed and used by the various processes taught within this workbook.

27. I: The Corners of The Mouth
Nourish the Spirit as Well as the Body

Mountain Over Thunder

When one learns to feed their Being with the energy of the Universe or Cosmos (God-Source), anything is possible. Energy is abundant for all needs, and manifestation is spontaneous. Often, simply a thought creates reality.

It is this Creative Energy flowing through the body and focused by the mind and projected by the will that makes all things possible.

Nurturing others, as the Universe nurtures you, will lead to success as those in a position of power become generous mentors.

Waxing Moon: To build good relations while invigorating yourself and others. Create a "Win, Win, situation."

Waning Moon: To prevent the competition with, or the jealousy of others, from ruining your chances of success.

28. TA KUO: Preponderance of the Great
Excess Creates Unbalance, Change Is Therefore Imminent

Lake Over Wind

When unused abundance becomes unused excess, collapse and failure are imminent. But the wise know that distribution of the excess brings further prosperity and prolonged success.

Waxing Moon: To create (or to build an excessive condition in something) the knowledge or awareness of and excess condition for future distribution.

Waning Moon: To promote the wise distribution of any excess and thus prolong the life of the situation, business, etc.

29. K'AN: Abysmal
The Abyss: Hardships, Darkness, and Danger

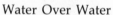

Water Over Water

If there is uncertainty and hardship, accompanied by the real possibility of danger within your immediate surroundings, overcome such situations by obtaining confidence, focus, guidance, and the proper attitude in which to confront this danger from within.

Waxing Moon: To build protection from danger, use K'an, in conjunction with Ta Ch'u (for added energy), Li (the honest and good prevail), and Shih Ho (to prosper in the situation). Carefully add any other hexagrams that the situation may warrant.

Place your hexagrams within the 12th zodiac House of Pisces, (secret enemies) or the 7th zodiac House of Libra (open enemies).

For added protection, burn a blue or white candle as a catalyst (see appendix).

Waning Moon: To destroy the efforts of those who would harm you, place your hexagrams in the 12th or 7th zodiac house as specified above. Use Ta Ch'u (destroying your opponent's energy) and write down the name of your aggressor if you can. Next, place K'an and Ku (to destroy your opponent's efforts) next to Ta Ch'u, along with the aggressor's name, within your chosen Zodiac House.

For added protection, burn a gray candle as a catalyst.

30. LI: Clinging Fire
Radiance and Prosperity Manifests from the God-Self

Fire Over Fire

When a situation hinges upon two key individuals, where one cannot act without the other, this is Li; where one is separate yet dependent.

Li is also the hexagram of the Spiritual Teacher, the Illuminator, the Shaman, Witch, Sage, and Magickan. For those that use Li in earnest, all mysteries unfold, all power is made available, and nothing is impossible. Li is the burning fire of illumination; without Li the Kundalini does not rise and wisdom cannot be. *Waxing Moon*: Use Li with Ta Ch'u (potential energy). In this way, you will be building not only power, but the secrets to knowing how to use that power wisely.

For the mundane world, use Li to gain the cooperation of someone who could help you in some way. Li also builds great success, for the honest and the dishonest cannot prevail against them.

Waning Moon: To dissipate or lessen the effect of a magickal spell or to negate the energy of those magickally irresponsible.

For the mundane world, to remove a key person, allowing for a replacement. This may be a beneficial or destructive action.

Be careful how you use Li, as you do not want the dishonest to prevail over the honest. That is why it is best to use Li only on the waxing moon unless you are sure of what you are doing.

31. HSIEN: Influences of Courtship
Young Lovers: Wooing, Attraction and Courtship

Lake Over Mountain

Hsien speaks of falling into love naturally. This is a true love and an attraction without superficial trappings, schemes, or designs. This is a bonding between two souls, not a contrived marriage of convenience for power, money, and physical pleasure.

Waxing Moon: Use on the waxing Moon for all matters of the heart where strengthening, building, beginning, or proving love is required.

Waning Moon: When relations no longer serve the good of both parties, it is often best to let love fade so that new relations may be started.

32. HENG: Enduring or Continuing
Adapt and Mold to the Needs of Another: Become as One

Thunder Over Wind

As two halves of a coin are of no value unless united, so it is with partnerships, marriage, and one's own spiritual peace.

Heng is used to strengthen bonds already formed and that are already working well. It renews and perpetuates what has already been started.

Waxing Moon: To build on what is already been started.

Waning Moon: To tear down that which you no longer desire, or that no longer serves in one's best interest.

33. TUN: Yield or Retreat
The Wise may yield or retreat, thus saving their energy for another day when all things are to their advantage

Heaven Over Mountain

To the Westerner, the thought of retreat or withdrawal is a thought of cowardice. To the enlightened mind, retreating, withdrawing, or yielding at the proper time is wise indeed.

This tactic allows one the opportunity to gather strength, wisdom, and power, and to await a more favorable time to act.

Waxing Moon: To freeze the moment or situation to allow time to retreat, regroup, and think out a plan of action.

Waning Moon: To prevent the retreat or withdrawal of someone or something in any situation or action.

34. TA CHUNG: Power of the Great
At this time you are gifted with great power and
strength, but if you abuse this gift it will be taken
from you

Thunder Over Heaven

Having the opportunity to wield great power and strength (also magick) is not only a rare gift, but a test of your character as well.

The Universe, however, has found you worthy enough to test how you will use this gift. How you use or abuse this power will determine what is gifted to you or taken from you in the future.

Waxing Moon: To build wisdom and to build resistance to the temptations for its misuse is the proper use of this hexagram.

Waning Moon: Use Ta Chung on the waning moon to banish all desires, situations, persons, words, emotions, or thoughts that would conflict with the proper use of this hexagram. Open any doors that were closed to you.

35. CHIN: Progress or Gain
From the proper use of Power and Strength springs the
further gifts of Recognition and Enlightenment

Fire Over Earth

This hexagram represents reward for virtuous efforts. It
speaks of good luck, fortune, fame, rapid gain, progress, and
effortless advancement.

This hexagram also speaks of such good fortune as a test from
the Universe. Falling to the temptation of misusing your good
fortune by selfishly harming another will bring loss of all that
has been given to you.

Waxing Moon: To protect your good fortune and reputation and
to obtain or maintain wisdom.

Waning Moon: Use to repel disaster, error, or anyone that might
tempt you into abusing your gifts.

36. MING I: A Darkening of the Light
This is the time of the selfish, self-serving, crooked,
corrupt, dishonored, immoral, dangerous, and jealous
ones of society to rule

Earth Over Fire

As the Moon waxes and wanes, so the cycles of life undulate
from prosperity and comfort to times that threaten your good
fortune with poverty, despair, and discomfort.

Often this is an unjust time with people who are cold and
heartless. To survive such arduous times with your integrity
intact, become as a reed in the wind; bend, but do not break by
compromising your morals and good judgment.

This is a time for patience and waiting. Reserve your strength, and what seems like insurmountable problems will fade as future prosperity takes over.

Waxing Moon: To build strength, courage, and power over those that would harm you. To provide a proper time for action and thus victory.

Waning Moon: Use Ming I to diminish the power and energy of those that are crooked, corrupt, and seeking your downfall.

37. CHIA JEN: The Clan or Family
Peace, Harmony, and Good Family Relations

Wind Over Fire

Chia Jen relates to a happy family life where each member has individual responsibilities that promote and support the well being of the family in some way; where all members are loved equally, each knowing their place and their responsibilities to the whole. It is in this way that all family members prosper (equally from the benefits of their work), emotionally, physically, and mentally.

Waxing Moon: To build a loving and harmonious home atmosphere. To gain wisdom, insight, and compassion on the problems of individual members of the family. Lead others in the family and make them feel important.

Waning Moon: Use to diminish family poverty on all levels; from squabbles, problems, and insecurities to brawling.

38. K' UEI: Opposition or Differences
Opposing Beliefs, Goals, and Views Can Work Harmoniously

Fire Over Lake

K'uei is the perfect hexagram for bringing opposing goals and views together into a single and focused effort to meet a desired end.

Whether in the workplace or at home, K'uei will be invaluable when squabbles from varying personalities create disharmony, and goals cannot be reached due to differences of opinion.

Waxing Moon: To build harmony between specified individuals and to unite all in the efforts toward a single goal.

Waning Moon: To dispel existing disharmony and hard feelings between individuals that cause underlying problems. Or K'uei, if used improperly, can actually be used to cause friction and disharmony between specified individuals. So use this hexagram wisely.

39. CHIEN: Obstacles or Obstructions
A Time to Seek the Aid of Others and of Healing

Water Over Mountain

Chien is the hexagram of blocks, obstacles, or obstructions. As with all blocked conditions, this is a time to rest and restore one's energy. Seek the wise counsel of your higher nature. Consider seeking the advise of those wiser than yourself, you might even consider joining forces.

Waxing Moon: To build or create blocks for others or to gain strength to overcome obstacles now in your path. Use Chien to gather supporters or partners and wise counsel that can help you.

Waning Moon: Chien is perfect when used to dissolve all blocks, obstacles, and obstructions standing in your way of success. This includes people, situations, and financial barriers.

40. HSIEH: Deliverance or Liberation
This is the time to regain freedom and happiness from
oppression, restraint, and hard times

Thunder Over Water

This hexagram advises that a difficult task is at hand, but do not despair, this is short lived and leads to much happiness and freedom. Timing is indicated here so do not put off the matter at hand.

The initial stress of facing down and righting the situation passes quickly as the joy, happiness, and prosperity catch hold. Your success is imminent.

Waxing Moon: Use Hsieh when facing any unpleasant person or situation where you need an edge.

Waning Moon: Hsieh used on the waning moon can further dissolve the power of those opposing you. Simply name them and place this hexagram over their name or their picture, then place their name or picture within the zodiac house of your choice (usually the 7th or 12th is used here).

41. SUN: Decrease or Decline
Seeking to donate to the common good and prosperity
of others results in a temporary decline or decrease
for yourself

Mountain Over Lake

Sometimes, to prosper, it is wise to donate one's time, money, and effort to a common good. While this temporarily strains and taxes the donating individual's freedom, money, and spirits, it will ultimately lead to recognition and benefit.

Sun can also be seen as giving the opportunity to prove one's self in some matter. This might mean that you would be working for less pay than you expected or hoped for until you have proven your worth. But do not think of Sun as complete misfortune, it is not. Actually it is the opportunity and doorway into far better future prospects; but, to make room for new and better things in life, some things must die or be lost to us.

Other examples of declines and decreases that can seem bad at first glance, but can lead to better days: lay-offs, bankruptcies, bank reorganizations, volunteer work, civic work, pay cuts (due to poor company income), etc.

Waxing Moon: Sun is an extremely complex hexagram. Used on the waxing moon, it can create a condition of loss and self-sacrifice. It can also be used to protect one from the excessive effects of such loss due to hexagram #42, Increase.

Be careful how you use Sun, be specific in your desires and where you place it within the zodiac.

Waning Moon: Use to avoid being asked to make sacrifice without just compensation. Avoid any or further losses altogether. #41, Sun, used on the waning moon will create #42, I.

The effects of using Sun on the waning moon are not as powerful as using #42, I, on a waxing moon, but it is very good for emergencies and when a waxing moon is not available.

42. I: Benefit or Increase
From Self-sacrifice Comes Recognition and Prosperity

Wind Over Thunder.

As was seen in hexagram 41, the need for self-sacrifice or inconvenience brought decrease. However, I shows that any losses suffered have now healed and a position of prosperity, respect, and power has been attained.

I also cautions not to abuse this time of good fortune by dishonest conduct, or dishonor and losses will be immediately forthcoming.

Waxing Moon: When you have suffered a loss of any kind (popularity, money, happiness, prestige, etc.) or have been seriously inconvenienced to the point of loss, use I to recover and regain your stability.

Waning Moon: I used on a waning moon will create #41, Sun, and a declining or decreasing condition.

43. KUAI: Breakthrough or Resolution
Expose and Remove Corruption, But with Caution

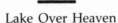

Lake Over Heaven

Kuai is the hexagram to use for exposing corruption, deceit, and enemies. Kuai offers an opportunity for cleansing yourself and your surroundings of undesirable influences.

Using caution during this time is essential, as you may experience real danger for your honesty and knowledge.

To properly and safely deal with the situation will require a calm, cool, and unemotional composure, and knowing your facts. Do not be tempted to meet hostility with revenge and anger. It is only through quiet calm that you will be the ultimate victor.

Waxing Moon: Use to build protection and power against those you wish to expose, and who would do you harm.

Waning Moon: To diminish the energy and power of your enemies over you.

44. KOU: Coming to Meet or Temptation
Present Circumstances Create Temptation and Danger

Heaven Over Wind

There will always be times when circumstances create moments of temptation. These moments can be avoided, but seldom are. These temptations, no matter how brief or fleeting, can lead us into ultimate disaster, ruin, humiliation, and despair.

Whether your temptation is gambling, sex, money, or other compulsions outside of your normal character, Kou is the hexagram of choice.

Waxing Moon: Place Kou in the zodiac house (or houses) where you are weakest and open to temptation. Concentrate on building up your resistance to the temptation or to hide an indiscretion.

Waning Moon: To reduce or banish the effects altogether of those persons or situations that create your temptations, place Kou in the appropriate house.

Within those houses write the name of your tempters and what it is you want them to stop doing. Such as, "Mr. Tompkins, stop trying to seduce me." Place this in whichever zodiac house applies to Mr. Tompkins: If he is your boss, Capricorn; if Mr. Tompkins is another employee, Virgo.

45. TS'UI: Assembling or Massing Together
Coming Together for a Single Purpose Creates Success

Lake Over Earth

Ts'ui is the hexagram of large groups working cooperatively and harmoniously toward a common goal or purpose.

Waxing Moon: Use to create harmony and single mindedness toward a common goal or single endeavor.

Waning Moon: Ts'ui, if used on the waning moon, will cause discontent, arguments, and ultimate failure of any common goal or project.

46. SHENG: Pushing Upward or Advancement
Advancement Commensurate with Abilities, Brings Prosperity and Self Esteem

Earth Over Wind

Sheng is the perfect hexagram for those seeking a better job, a promotion, or any type of advancement. Be aware, though, that Sheng will not help you if you are not already qualified. This particular hexagram aids those qualified for the position they are seeking.

Waxing Moon: Use Sheng to gain any position for which you are qualified. This will give you an edge over your competition.

Waning Moon: When used on a waning moon, Sheng will lessen the chances of your competition. Simply write down your competition's name on a piece of paper and place this hexagram atop the name. Then, place the name in the House of Capricorn (Professions) or Aquarius (your wishes, for or toward the competition).

47. K'UN: Oppression or Adversity
A Tired, Worn Down Condition Creates Difficulties

Lake Over Water

Pacing one's self is important for success, to take on too much results in overload, burn-out, and loss of credibility when one cannot perform properly. Taking on too little to reserve one's strength creates a reputation for laziness or lack of ability.

The solution is to moderate actions until strength and power are regained. It is vital that you do not express firm opinions or complain, as it will lead to discord. Listen rather than talk.

Waxing Moon: This hexagram, used on a waxing moon, builds a weariness; unless you specify that you are building energy and power against what this hexagram represents.

Waning Moon: Use K'un on a waning moon to banish ill health, stress, or any other problem that is causing your present condition.

48. CHING: The Well or Life Source
Draw Water from the Wellspring of Life and Wisdom

Water Over Wind

Use Ching when meditating or seeking wisdom, guidance or answers to important questions for others. All questions lie within the scope of Ching, which emphasizes wisdom sought for helping others (social or many others).

Waxing Moon: Building wisdom is within the scope of Ching on a waxing moon. It can also be used to contact inner teachers or guides. The only stipulation is that the wisdom sought be ultimately for helping another.

Waning Moon: An excellent time to help others tear down and rid themselves of preconceived ideas, prejudices, and erroneous teachings from religious or social structures. Ching is perfect for the teacher or philosopher.

49. KO: To Revolt, Change or Molt
Deceptive Ruling Breeds Corruption and Revolution

Lake Over Fire

Anyone facing corruption will need Ko. It is a hexagram for conquering corruption and setting all things right.

Use Ko in conjunction with other empowering hexagrams for protection, strength, power, and ultimate success.

Waxing Moon: To empower and conquer.

Waning Moon: To weaken those opposing you.

50. TING: The Cauldron of Universal Order
At Peace with the Goddess, At Peace with the World

Fire Over Wind

Ting is the Cauldron of Life. And, as such, all good flows from Her. All needs are answered. This is the hexagram of long forgotten Women's Mysteries and magick. Meditate upon Ting to contact Goddess energy and protection.

Waxing Moon: Protection, health, wealth, prosperity, and Women's Mysteries.

Waning Moon: Banishing all that does not serve one's highest and best good.

51. CHEN: Arousing or to Shock
Swiftly Occurring Action Catches One Off Guard

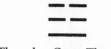

Thunder Over Thunder

Chen speaks of someone or some force, perhaps nature (or a magickan using magick) acting in a swift, aggressive, and unpredictable way. The effect creates surprise and possibly danger, shock, fear, and terror.

Waxing Moon: To move swiftly and seize power and control with enough surprise that no one can stand against you. Liken Chen to a corporate war where one corporation is suddenly taken over by an another, "A Hostile Takeover."

Waning Moon: To prevent hostile actions or aggressors from swiftly taking over any situation.

52. KEN: Keeping Still or Going Within
Seeking Wisdom from One's Inner Source

Mountain Over Mountain

Seek the higher guidance of self at this time. It is only by contacting your Higher Being that peace, balance, and truth are restored within your life. This will bring renewed vitality and happiness.

This hexagram is best used to gauge the inner balance and path through its use in meditation.

Waxing Moon: When you feel out of balance, lost, indecisive, and out of harmony with your surroundings, ground and center your energy using Ken in the following zodiac houses: #1 Aries (Physical Imbalances), #3 Gemini (Mental or Intellectual Imbalances), #9 Sagittarius (Inner Quests, Religious Aspirations, The God/dess Self).

Waning Moon: Place Ken where blocks or difficulties may be plaguing you. The answers to your problems and obstacles will come and the situations will resolve themselves.

53. CHIEN: Steady Progress or Development
Follow the Natural Order to Good Fortune

```
▬▬▬▬▬
▬▬▬▬▬
▬▬ ▬▬
▬▬▬▬▬
▬▬ ▬▬
▬▬ ▬▬
```

Wind Over Mountain

There are those that seek success through aggression and short cuts, while others slowly and with deliberate calmness plod onward, reaping the rewards of their efforts.

While the safest and slowest route may seem unexciting or unglamorous for many, it is the surest way to harmony, happiness, and ultimate success.

Waxing Moon: Use to build a strong and solid foundation for success and prosperity in life.

Waning Moon: Use to banish all that does not serve your highest and best good. Chien is particularly good to use on the waning moon. It clears away large obstacles and eases you along your path with fewer problems. Further, it assures that you will not be overcome by blocks, possibly endangering your goals.

54. KUEI MEI: The Marrying Maiden or Subordination
Adapting to the Unavoidable Leads to Success

```
▬▬ ▬▬
▬▬ ▬▬
▬▬▬▬▬
▬▬ ▬▬
▬▬▬▬▬
▬▬▬▬▬
```

Thunder Over Lake

At times, we find ourselves in a situation or a circumstance, which fate or karma has meted out for our education and experience, that is unavoidable.

Such lessons as described by Kuei Mei are between people in relationships that are permanent, such as a business and its owner, two business partners, spouses, employer, and employee, or any relationship where one party is dominant over the other and expects the subordinate to be actively submissive on all levels.

For some, such a situation is of no particular consequence and the individuals learn to adapt. Others, though, find the situation or circumstance intolerable, almost smothering.

Kuei Mei says the secrets to success in such a situation lie in adapting and working within the restraints or confines of the relationship. To fight or try to change this type of relationship only brings heartache, loss, and ultimate sorrow.

Waxing Moon: Use to build power, strength, and wisdom that allows you to bend, but not break, within your present circumstance.

Waning Moon: Use Kuei Mei to reveal the way out of your current situation and provide an alternate path to happiness. Kuei Mei can also be used on the waning moon to lessen the effects of such a situation.

55. FENG: Abundance at its Fullest
The Peak of Abundance Is Short Lived

Thunder Over Fire

All things work in their proper and natural order; as decline is followed by growth, so prosperity is followed by need. The wise know how to take advantage of this moment of abundance while preparing for the lesser times to come.

For that reason, when using Feng, realize its effects are potent but short lived, and be prepared for what would naturally come next.

Waxing Moon: Rise to whatever zenith is possible within the situation you are working with. Whether money, power, or matters of the heart, your luck runs strong at this time.

Waning Moon: Use to lessen and better control the effects of losses in any matter.

56. LU: The Traveler or Wanderer
The Need for Travel Can Cause Vulnerability

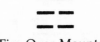

Fire Over Mountain

There are times when travel is a must to assure one's success. It is during these times that one is most vulnerable to accidents, falling prey to criminal victimization, and falling victim to the incompetence of others.

Lu explains that many problems of the weary traveler can be remedied with foresight, thus avoiding anger, anxiety, and many other travel problems as well.

However, using Lu in talisman form, along with other powerful hexagrams, will help one to avoid the unforeseen and unplanned difficulties of travel.

Waxing Moon: Use to build protection from the unforeseen or unplanned situations that plague the tired traveler.

Waning Moon: Use to reduce or banish the dangers often met with on trips.

57. SUN: Gentle Penetration Influence
Non-Aggressive Action and Organization Creates Fortune

Wind Over Wind

Non-aggressive action and organization will bring new opportunities to prove your worth. Gently, seek the wise counsel of those more experienced and you will begin to make progress which results in acknowledgment of your achievements with monetary advancement.

Waxing Moon: Sun is particularly good to use if you are a new employee anxious to prove yourself and get into the network of company achievers. Sun is excellent for non-aggressive individuals or a situation requiring a gentle but effective touch.

Waning Moon: Use Sun to dissolve any problems or blocks you may be having.

58. TUI: Joyous Lake
A Cheerful and Polite Attitude Leads to Success

Lake Over Lake

The hexagram of Tui is versatile and can be used in all areas of your life (especially for popularity) where you wish to be noticed. By encouraging those around you, you cause others to take an interest in you.

A sincere and cheerful attitude attracts new opportunities, new friends (that are extremely loyal), and recognition for your efforts.

Tui is perfect for anyone who is required to meet or greet the public and is therefore ideally suited to politics, business, entertainment, sales, and family life.

A word of caution when using Tui: Too much popularity can lead to ego problems, social addictions, and destruction of all your work. Use moderation with Tui. Remember, too much fun can be just as bad as not enough.

Waxing Moon: Building strong communications and people skills, Tui creates deep and loyal bonds of friendship and popularity wherever it is placed.

Waning Moon: Tui opens doors to social, political, and family functions that were otherwise closed to you. This is possible due to the strong social magnetism that surrounds those who use Tui as a Talisman.

59. HAUN: Dispersing and Reuniting
Blocked Energy Creates Isolation

Wind Over Water

When humans become blocked or cut off from the Higher Sources that we refer to as God or Goddess, they feel alone, without answers, and powerless, and fail in life's endeavors.

When the individual goes within to rediscover, open up, or clear away these energy blocks (blocked chakras), communication with the God or Goddess is again opened. Energy, for manifestation, again flows freely.

It is at this point in life that the individual once again finds that abundance is only a thought or desire away. Life is once more worth living as good fortune is everywhere, while wisdom is no longer a matter of deep effort, but comes naturally.

Waxing Moon: After dissolving all energy blocks, cords, and unhealthy conditions within your being upon the waning moon, begin to rebuild what you want. This is generally health, wealth, wisdom, and prosperity. All are now possible, as you are reconnected to your God or Goddess source, and to the energy you need to manifest your goals.

Waning Moon: Huan is a powerful talisman for clearing blocks, cords, and foreign energies that may be preventing you from achieving spiritual enlightenment and earthly success.

60. CHIEH: Limitations or to Regulate
Difficult Times are Endured with Restrictions

Water Over Lake

Times of hardship appear throughout our lives and serve as the natural rhythm or cycles of life. Knowing this makes one just a little wiser and better off than those who fight against life. Those who understand that nature's cycles are simply energy patterns that can be influenced by the mind (magick) and proper preparation, seldom find such times unbearable.

Difficult times, therefore, can be short lived and survival imminent with foresight and the regulation of emotions, desires, actions, services, expenditures, and productions. So, too, the cycles will respond to magick.

Waxing Moon: Place Chieh wherever you wish to limit or regulate a person, place, thing, object, action, or act.

Chieh, used with other hexagrams of power and protection, can protect one from depressions, recessions, and losses, depending on one's needs.

Waning Moon: Use to banish hard times, ill luck, and negative energy that causes any kind of limitation. Use Chieh in court battles over laws and regulations that are too severe. Chieh will diminish the power of those you oppose and help you to demonstrate your grievances. Of course, you will want to add several other hexagrams with Chieh to ensure your power and victory in such a legal battle.

61. CHUNG FU: Inner Truth from the Higher Self
Become One with Another and Understand

Wind Over Lake

Chung Fu is the hexagram for obtaining power over those who cannot see any truth but their own. To do this, Chung Fu states that you should become as one with your opponent or enemy. This is done with an open heart and mind and without prejudice. Only in this way can one make an unbiased determination of the situation and plan for future action, if any.

Should action be required, then you now have a clear and unclouded appraisal of the situation and full knowledge of all weaknesses and strengths of your enemy or opponent. Being armed with such information weakens the opposing forces, allowing no room for victory.

Waxing Moon: Use to conquer an opponent through their own weaknesses by placing Chung Fu within the appropriate zodiac house. Use Chung Fu to hide or cloak your activities until your mission is complete.

Waning Moon: Breaking down the resistance of an enemy or opponent is best done on the waning moon. In this case, Chung Fu could be used to scatter the energy, power, and influence the opposition may hold over any situation.

62. HSIAO KUO: Small and Gentle
The Little Things Loom Largest in Life

Thunder Over Mountain

There are times when quick and aggressive actions are necessary and called for in life (#28 Preponderance of the Great). Yet there are other times when a full force attack is not desired, possible, or even feasible. Hsiao Kuo is then the hexagram of choice.

Hsiao Kuo should be used for small victories and issues where overt aggression would bring certain failure. When using this hexagram, pay attention to detail; it is the small, minute, seemingly innocent matters that count and can aid your success.

Do not push forward when using Hsiao Kuo; bide your time and allow this hexagram to work for you. Accept and work on your small and seemingly minor victories. These are what will lead you to success.

Liken the covert actions of Hsiao Kuo to drops of water onto a large stone. Soon the rock is so weakened that it wears down to nothing, creating success and victory for the weaker and less obviously powerful water.

Waxing Moon: Use Hsiao Kuo in situations where loud aggressive or overt actions would be unwise and inappropriate. This hexagram can also be used as a talisman to block others from undermining authority and power.

Waning Moon: Employers can use Hsiao Kuo to rid themselves of troublemakers and to neutralize their destructive and eroding energy.

63. CHI CHI: After Completion or the End
Victory Cycles to Lethargy and Ultimately Decay

Water Over Fire

Goals have been met, power and prosperity achieved, a cycle is ending and a new one beginning. The new cycle brings complacency, indifference, and, all too often, irresponsibility and laziness. This situation will ultimately lead to decay and thus the cycle will start anew for those who do not know how to stop or lessen the effects of such cycles.

For those aware of such cycles: With success achieved satisfaction in a task well done can be enjoyed. Remain alert, though, for minor tasks that will be required to maintain that success, and not become lazy or complacent. It is best to take care of all small projects, for it is this way that your success will last and be assured.

Waxing Moon: Use to maintain and protect what has been hard won and lessen or block the cycle of decrease.

Waning Moon: Use to lessen the effects of rot and decay that would jeopardize all that has been won or acquired.

64. WEI CHI: Before Completion or the End
Order from Disorder

Fire Over Water

Wei Chi can be likened to a fairy tale where the hero or heroine is in the midst of battle and trying desperately to bring about a new order of peace and tranquility.

So it is with any situation where you find yourself locked within the middle of change and need the momentum and courage to see the issue or circumstance through to the conclusion. In such cases, Wei Chi can help, with the addition of other hexagrams as the situation or circumstance indicates.

The most important thing to remember is that Wei Chi is used just "before the end or conclusion" of any matter of importance. It fortifies, strengthens, and helps one to achieve order out of the present disorder. It helps to ring in a new and more prosperous cycle.

Waxing Moon: Use to protect one from the dangers or misfortunes of bringing about needed change (restoring order or justice from chaos and injustice).

Build wisdom and clarity where the situation warrants and display the proper course of action to be taken for victory.

Waning Moon: Diminishes and banishes those that seek to retain the old order or disorder of things. Wei Chi can be used to oust those in power who are corrupt or no longer efficient in their positions.

Chapter 8 Quiz

Select the hexagram that best fits the description.
1. To remove misfortune from yours or another's life, and replace this negativity with abundance.
2. To find or create a true love.
3. To free yourself from major problems and stress.

4. To renew interest in a dwindling love relationship.
5. To break or weaken an enemy.

Answers

1. #11 T'ai banishes ill fortune and replaces it with good fortune.
2. #31 Hsien creates true and unselfish love.
3. #32 Heng liberates and aids in problem solving.
4. #40 Chieh renews love.
5. #23 Po weakens adverse forces and allows final victory for the attacker.

9

Runes

Definition of the Rune: A Rune is an ideograph. A pictorial representation of an idea or concept.

A Brief History of Runes: Runes date back well into prehistory and appear mysteriously all over Europe. Yet, serious occult scholars, runeologists, and archaeologists are hard pressed to state the exact origins, meanings, and use of runes by early civilizations.

The general acceptance is, however, that the Elder Futhark, being composed of twenty-four Runes, is the fundamental or base of all other present-day runic systems.

It has been speculated that the Teutonic peoples may have borrowed the Elder Futhark around three hundred to one hundred B.C.E. from an even earlier and more obscure source.

What is known is that the Runes were used in magickal rites and it is not uncommon to find dwellings, knives, cooking ware, and other personal items decorated with various magickal combinations of runic scripts denoting, health, wealth, protection, fertility, and prosperity.

Our objective for including the Runes in a talisman text is to familiarize you with another system of divination that, as in the case of the Tarot and the I Ching, can be incorporated into an effective and potent talisman.

On the following pages are listed the twenty-four Runes most commonly used today. Each has be annotated with an explanation as to its key concepts and general meanings along with suggested uses on both the waxing and waning moon.

1. Fehu

Fehu, Foeh
Sound Value: F

Rune of: Raw power.

Key Concept: The availability of power for the manifestation of wealth.

Mundane Meanings: Livestock, wealth, and power.

General Meanings: All matters of prosperity and wealth. Comfort, fertility, reproduction, and social status. The protection of wealth from theft, loss of job, injury, or chicanery. Good fortune in all money matters and earned income. The building of wealth through one's own efforts. Fehu is also used to expedite any situation or circumstance.

Magickal Use: The Sending or Destroying Rune; to send magickal power where needed to strengthen surrounding Runes, a situation, or circumstance. Magickal Power unleashed as a wildly destructive or constructive force upon any affair or person.

The channeling and projection of this force clears the chakras, cleans the aura, and enhances all psychic abilities. This allows one to easily manifest or create one's own reality with an unlimited supply of Universal Energy.

Waxing Moon: Use to build wealth and fortune. Fehu can also be used to block anyone from stealing your money, or hindering your abilities when used on the waxing moon.

Waning Moon: To weaken or banish those persons or obstacles that would hinder your ability to earn.

This Rune used on the waning moon can delay or eliminate lay-offs when used within the House of Employers, #10 Capricorn.

If used in Capricorn on a waning moon, follow up this process up on the next New Moon (Waxing Moon) by using Eolh (Defense-Protection), Tir (Victory-Warrior), Beorc (New Growth or Regeneration), Wunjo (Happy Endings or outcome) in the House of Occupation and Service, #6 Virgo.

2. Uruz

Uruz, Ur
Sound Value: U

Rune of: Harnessing, or the shaping of power.

Key Concept: The Act of Manifesting; to bring forth form from the formless state in accordance with one's will.

Mundane Meanings: Wild bison, ox, aurochs, rain, physical strength, and power.

General Meanings: Newness, birth; to open doors that will offer new opportunities, avenues, and potential growth. To expedite any matter. Universal or Cosmic Energy. Unlimited strength, power, and vitality. All that is wild and untamed within ourselves, surroundings, or others.

The Vital Essence of life, healing, freedom, action, courage, the body, ego, boldness, and fierceness.

Womanhood, manhood, rights of passage and self transmutation, and lust. To grow, adapt and harmonize with one's environment, to heal all.

Uruz also has dominion over brutality, rashness, callousness, violence, and sexual excesses or perversion.

Magickal Use: Healing, through the use of magick (energy manipulation via the will). The special use of the Earth's energy and Her magnetic fields for use in Ritual, Earth Magick, Shamanism. To obtain wisdom in the use of Earth Magick and early Shamanistic practices.

Waxing Moon: Use to heal or manifest change by sheer force of the will. Use Uruz to swiftly shape or mold any situation to your desire. Add Uruz to other Runes for added strength, energy, and power wherever needed.

Waning Moon: Use to completely destroy an unwanted situation. Use Uruz with caution on a waning moon, as it is not only powerful, but can be unpredictable, wild, and unruly.

3. Thurisaz

Thurisaz, Thorn
Sound Value: th

Rune of: Power directed by sheer force of will.

Key Concepts: The capacity to wield the raw powers of destruction and self defense into and through the body for a desired end.

Mundane Meanings: Thorn, sharpness.

General Meanings: The resistance breaker, the protector, the block or barrier breaker, great powers of expansion, strength, sharpness, cruelty, stealth, luck, and the power to destroy one's enemies.

To create love and new beginnings in life. To solve problems. To control the evil, malice, hatred, and lies, and for the purging of undesirable characters (both men and women) from your surroundings.

Directed by the will, this powerful Rune creates action (destruction) or non-action (protective barrier) in accord with one's desires. It is a Rune to be used for the protection of yourself and loved ones.

Magickal Meanings: For the breaking up of love magick and curses. To create or gain the upper hand in any love affair; to perform love magick and control the heart of the one you love. Use this Rune to bind others to your will and to support other Runes in your magickal endeavors.

To prevent others from hindering your magick. Fine for all cases of magickal self-defense, aggression, and manifestation of the will.

The power held within this Rune can be projected outward by the will. The actual effects of your mental projection will be determined by any surrounding Runes, and which Zodiac House you choose to work in. This Rune works most effectively in Talisman Magick.

Waxing Moon: Use on a waxing moon to create a strong defensive and protective barrier around one's self, something, or someone. Thurisaz strengthens the aura and sharpens the senses; adds luck to any situation.

Waning Moon: When used on the waning moon, Thurisaz will completely destroy whatever tasks it has been directed to. Once set into motion, this Rune will do its work even though you have second thoughts. Therefore, use this Rune wisely and cautiously. Use Thurisaz to break down barriers on the waning moon.

4. Ansuz

Ansuz, Os
Sound Value: A

Rune of: Mental agility, self expression, and all forms of communications.

Key Concepts: Magick; the Message Rune; channeling the Old and Ancient Ones.

Mundane Meaning: Mouth or God.

General Meanings: This Rune will destroy or shatter any attempts at physical abuse or any force being directed toward you or someone you love. The power and essence of the ancestor or god. Spiritual ecstasy, signals, gifts, and warnings; the supraconscious, conscious and unconscious mind.

Education, scholarship, teaching, speaking, writing (communications in all forms), negotiations, debates, dealing with the public or media, politicians, leaders, soldiers, warriors, wise leadership, and wise advice or counsel.

Ensures luck and confidence in all matters dealing with people; and promotes freedom while destroying prejudice, ignorance, and tyranny.

Magickal Use: The Rune of charisma and personal magnetism through the power of communication. Good for anyone in competition with others or requiring success through the power of communications. Whether you're a singer, politician, disk jockey, TV anchor, writer, or lecturer, this Rune will favorably enchant your audience.

It also controls the secrets of magickal knowledge, incantations, enchantments, mediumship, channeling, banishing, exorcisms, ancestor worship, and religious philosophy. For possessions, hauntings, and poltergeists, use with Thurisaz-Power, Eihwaz-Banishing, and Beorc-Earth Mother, in Scorpio.

Waxing Moon: Use to build the magickal mind and body; For building a successful career in front of the public through any means of communication.

Waning Moon: Use to banish fears, ghosts, and undesirable influences in one's aura, home, and surroundings. Destroy tyranny, ignorance, and hatred within one's life.

5. Raidho

Raidho, Rad
Sound Value: R

Rune of: Justice served and travel.

Key Concepts: To journey, cosmic support of justice for the innocent.

Mundane Meanings: A wheel, to ride or travel, wheel of energy.

General Meanings: All modes of transportation.

To move (mentally or physically), in the proper direction. Satisfaction, protection, and luck in all matters of travel.

For anyone who enjoys racing or any sport that requires movement or travel, this Rune ensures safety and success.

To achieve victory and justice in any situation where you are in the right. Use Raidho in conjunction with Jera (Reaping What You Have Sown and all legal matters), when going to court.

Magickal Use: The channeling and harmonizing of the Higher, Middle and Lower selves; the path or road of the Kundalini. To learn and properly use the divine laws of Nature in magick.

The road back to peace, harmony, health, well being, prosperity, and balance, and the road back to the use of magick and the Old Gods and Goddesses.

Waxing Moon: Use to protect yourself or another when traveling, and to win where racing is concerned.

Waning Moon: Use to break up bad luck, fears or any blocks that concerns travel or movement.

6. Kaunaz

Kaunaz, Ken, Kenaz
Sound Value: K

Rune of: The Arts, magick, artists and craftspersons.

Key Concepts: The Creative Fires of Life and Passion, controlled by the will, results in progress, creation, sexual love, and new realities.

Mundane Meanings: Light, torch or sore (to burn or scorch, resulting in a sore).

General Meanings: Healthy sexual desires, passions and cravings. To create healthy, loving relationships, or friendly partnerships from otherwise hostile and destructive ones.

Protect valuables, health; build self-confidence, a positive attitude, new relationships, wisdom, and connect to one's own Higher Self and the Universe.

This Rune increases one's ability to create (magickally) and is therefore excellent for artists and craftspersons. It brings success, as those craftspersons who use its power find that no matter what is created, the object is transformed from the ordinary to the exceptional. This, of course, attracts success to the creator as people ponder just what it is about the object that makes it so special.

Magickal Use: All forms of love magick, and second only to Gebo in sex magick; healing and regeneration. Ideal for communing with the dead, and the creation of magickal objects of power.

Banishing! To banish all lower vibrations that cause harm in any way and to receive Universal Light that strengthens the aura and offers protection.

Waxing Moon: Use to bring in Universal Light Energy for protecting yourself, another, an object, or situation. This Rune is synonymous with the Universal Life Forces, and for that reason offers energy and protection to whatever lies close to it. Place it on any object or item or wherever protection is required.

Waning Moon: Kaunaz is best used first on the waning moon. Then use it once again on the waxing moon to bring in protection.

Banishings of all types are perfect for Kaunaz. From the lower vibrations of a discarnate (ghost) to ugly thought forms created by others, this Rune can be used to banish them all and cleanse your home, aura, and office.

Use Kaunaz to expose falsehoods and illusionary people, circumstances, and deceit.

7. Gebo

Gebo, Gyfu, Gifu
Sound Value: G

Rune of: Partnerships, unions, and groups

Key Concepts: The Opposite Polarities of Male and Female Energy. Combines the (magickal) energies of two or more toward a common goal.

Mundane Meaning: Gift (offering, present, donation, sacrifice).

General Meanings: Partnerships, popularity, inner peace, generosity to a point of self-sacrifice, forgiveness, gratitude, love, sexual union, peace and harmony between family members and loved ones. Rapport with co-workers, partners; a well-balanced self-image.

Magickal Use: The exchange of energies (Force/Power) between the Universe and humans as a gift (magick) from the God or Goddess for the progression of the species.

To become one with God or Goddess is to become wise, centered, balanced, and truly whole.

Union with the God or Goddess Self creating ecstasy, power, and well being. Sexual relations between partners for the purpose of sex magick—The Great Rite.

Where two or more come together for a magickal purpose, increased power will follow using this Rune.

Waxing Moon: Use Gebo in all matters of relationships and popularity. If you need a healthier self-image and better report with yourself and a God or Goddess, use Gebo.

Waning Moon: Rid yourself of unwanted or undesirable habits, conditions, or problems that keep others from liking you. Use Gebo to make others forget why they do not like you, and to open doors for new chances at relationships.

8. Wunjo

Wunjo, Wynn
Sound Value: W

The Rune of: Locking in a happy ending.

Key Concepts: Great joy.

Mundane Meaning: Balance creates joy.

General Meaning: When creating your talisman with Rune script, always be sure your last Rune is Wunjo. It ensures success and a happy ending to whatever you are manifesting.

Fulfillment, happiness, love, peace, camaraderie, fellowship, bonding, ties and contracts. Business (especially ownership), commerce, prosperity, glory, karmic rewards and personal satisfaction; attraction, magnetism, getting along with others. Laughter, parties, amusement parks, vacations, and holidays.

Wunjo can also be used against addictions, involuntary possessions (by discarnates), bondage, enchantments, and impracticality.

Magickal Use: For mastering the secrets of channeling the various types of energies and powers that make up our own world. The

Rune Wunjo can be used to harness and learn the various techniques required in harmonizing these energies.

Waxing Moon: Use to channel various types of energy and power for magickal use and practices. This Rune strengthens the ability to channel such energy and offers support for surrounding Runes. Use Wunjo to bind (bend) someone, something, or circumstance to your will. Create peace, harmony, and good will within any situation.

Build an enchantment and strengthen magickal success.

Waning Moon: Dispel or banish enchantments, undesired powers, or energies that no longer suit your purpose.

Wunjo can also be used to create serious problems between family members, partnerships, and couples. For that reason, it must be used with caution and clarity of purpose.

9. Hagalaz

N

Hagalaz, Hagalaz,
Sound Value: H

The Rune of: Progress, lessons successfully achieved.

Key Concepts: Slow and plodding; to work within and through constraints or limitations.

Mundane Meanings: Snow, hailstone, egg, or cosmic seed.

General Meanings: Any situation that limits or confines growth will yield to Hagalaz's slow but upward movement toward ultimate success. Where no positive or constructive movement was otherwise possible, Hagalaz will prevail. Extremes are often part of Hagalaz, the Rune Mother. Everything seems difficult when beginning and ending. Hagalaz can aid such difficult times.

Gain the support, trust, love, and loyalty of others, although interests may not be common ones. Applies to groups, families, clans, tribes, and governments.

Hagalaz also can be used against hardship, pain, suffering, loss, illness, natural or man made disasters, and bad weather.

Use in circumstances or situations where a calculated risk is involved, and luck is needed.

Magickal Use: The Rune of Afflictions and Hardships, Hagalaz signifies the realms of Hel, or the Underworld. It is the unification of opposites, the Rune of Transformation.

Waxing Moon: To influence, command, control or sway groups of people, use the 7th Zodiac House of Libra on a waxing moon.

Waning Moon: Destroy disease, ill health, suffering afflictions, heartache, disaster, and all bad luck.

10. Naudhiz

Nauthiz, Nied
Sound Value: N

The Rune of: Deliverance from need and distress.

Key Concepts: A time for cleansing, balancing, and harmonizing.

Mundane Meanings: Distress arising from severe need, yet having the capacity and capability to obtain those needs through the manipulation of Universal Power by will.

To understand your karma and the lessons required within this lifetime, yet knowing you have the power to alter or successfully work through these lessons with the aid of Naudhiz.

General Meanings: This Rune helps in all matters requiring good judgment and unbiased thinking; for goals, patience, and determination; to make amends and repay debts.

Use to cut through unwanted bonds that hold you to being a slave to a job, person, idea, or circumstance. Regain what is presently lacking in your life. Obtain the essentials that are needed to survive and all other needs in general; deprivation, poverty, starvation, emotion, and the inability to cope. Conquer self-programmed patterns of failure and destruction.

Magickal Use: The best Rune to use in magick or divination to find your perfect mate or lover. Also use this Rune to spice up your love life.

The sacred fires of spiritual and physical transformation create balance, order, and a keen magickal sense. This rune is also good for calling upon the spirit world and power animals.

Waxing Moon: Build new goals and directions; obtain what is lacking presently within your life.

Waning Moon: Break away from destructive patterns, bonds, circumstances, and people that no longer serve your best interest. Use this Rune to transform your life.

11. Isa

Isa, Is,
Sound Value: I

The Rune of: Freezing or halting.

Key Concepts: Standstill, that which blinds or impedes.

Mundane Meanings: Ice.

General Meaning: To overcome any situation or circumstance that is a plot, betrayal, lie, slippery, elusive, dangerous, deceitful, treacherous, and enchanting, or is illusionary.

To overcome distress, achieve goals, create protection, create beauty, solve conflict, create or tear down constraints or arguments, and to find or bring back a lover.

When used during the appropriate moon phase, Isa will halt destructive energies against you (waxing) and reverse this energy and return it to the sender (waning).

Magickal Use: Freeze or hold any situation allowing time to regroup and perform any necessary magick. Isa is very good when doing creative visualization, as it adds to inner clarity, vision, and communing with the Higher Self and inner worlds. Isa can be placed anywhere within the zodiac to expose deceit, plots, cover ups, or a false personality. In the case of the latter, Isa allows one to see through any magick that uses glamour, charm, or the allure of sexual seduction to accomplish its mission.

Waxing Moon: Use Isa, along with Jera (the Legal System), Raidho (Victory for the Just), and Wunjo (Happy Ending) when unjustly accused in a civil or criminal matter. Isa will give you time to prepare your defense on the waxing moon. In such a case, the best zodiac house to work from would be Libra #7 (Courts, Laws, Attorneys, and Justice).

Waning Moon: Using Isa on the waning moon releases any blocked or frozen condition and reverses any stagnant situation.

12. Jera

Jera, Jara,
Sound Value: J, Y, (A)

The Rune of: Reaping the rewards of what you have sown, and all legal matters

Key Concepts: Abundance and plenty.

Mundane Meanings: One complete season, or cycle of the year; harvest.

General Meanings: Abundance or reward from labors. Reaping the harvest of seeds sown. To create peace, harmony, and enlightenment within life. Sperm and egg, Jera is the Rune of fertility, quickening, and birth.

Magickal Use: A balance of Solar and Earth energies, ideal for creating the seeds of magickal desire. Place this Rune in any house where you want something to manifest, and watch it grow into a reality. Jera is ideal wherever you need a physical or tangible manifestation of some sort.

Waxing Moon: Use Jera when you must go to court to collect bad debts, keep creditors at bay, protect yourself from slander, or influence any legal case.

Waning Moon: Reverse the tide of events against you in court. Reverse any action brought about by another against you; legally return it to the sender.

13. Eihwaz

Eoh, Yr,
Sound Value: I or EI

The Rune of: Protection and banishing.
Key Concepts: Defense. The Tree of Wisdom, Life, and Death.
Mundane Meanings: A bow from the yew tree.
General Meanings: Keeper of the Sacred Fires; solid and strong, poisonous and deadly, no one can stand against the aversive powers of Eihwaz.

This is a very good Rune for the warrior or warrioress; self-defense, block or defeat another. Gain patience, foresight, competence, and wisdom.

Eihwaz is the Rune of right, or justice. It protects and empowers the innocent who seek success.

It transforms obstacles into stepping stones of success, and aids in business, finance, and management.

Magickal Use: To visit the underworld and learn the secrets of life, death, and reincarnation. To separate oneself from the physical body and travel with the astral to distant places and times.

To seek magickal wisdom and truth through initiation into the inner dimensional realms of magick.

Waxing Moon: Eihwaz is ideal for the mom and pop business trying to survive in a large corporate world. Eihwaz empowers, protects, and brings in successes against all odds.

Waning Moon: Banish destructive energies within one's life, aura, and surroundings.

14. Perdhro

Perthro, Peordh,
Sound Value: P

The Rune of: Gambling and risk taking.
Key Concepts: All secrets are the dominion of Perdhro.
Mundane Meanings: Gambling cup or box for lots or dice.
General Meanings: Abundance and the excesses that success can bring. Happiness, laughter, enjoyment; the foolhardy, inno-

cent, or childlike; addiction, gluttony, and all other excesses of
life; prostitution, lewdness, debauchery, mental illness, sexual
fantasies, and perversions; games of luck and all areas of risk
taking. Legacies, investments, finding lost objects, secrets, and
hidden treasure.

Magickal Use: Initiation into the magickal realms of the Unknowable, the Void and the meaning of the Phoenix. The secrets of
manipulating matter, energy, and fate in order to control your
own destiny.

Psychic death and spiritual rebirth and all forms of divination.
Waxing Moon: To win at gambling an other risk taking enter-
prises, consider using Perthro on the waxing moon in the Zodiac House of Leo #5, as it rules Gambling and Risks.

Waning Moon: To uncover ancient magickal secrets now lost to
humanity, Perdhro is the rune of choice and Scorpio, #8 (Occult
Secrets), is the house to use.

15. Eolh

Eihwaz, Algiz
Sound Value: Z

The Rune of: Divine protection.
Key Concepts: The Divine Shield of Protection, Protective Forces,
the Hero.
Mundane Meanings: Elk.
General Meanings: A Hero Rune, to protect and defend; increases
luck, loyalty, and communications with others; for control of
self, emotions and to bring about needed changes within one's
self; it protects all who use it and strengthens the aura.

The great power of this Rune is best applied when used to aid
others and to heal yourself. The selfish use of this Rune is said to
bring certain failure wherever used.

Magickal Meaning: This is the Rune of open communications
between humans and the Gods and Goddesses. It also links the
practitioner to any world he or she may wish to travel to and
explore in perfect safety.

Use this Rune to communicate with your spirit guides, or guardians in the inner planes.

Carry this Rune while traveling within the inner realm, astral projecting, or traveling within the mental body; it offers divine protection.

This Rune is perfect when placed upon the Magick Mirror. It increases the ability to see and safely travel into other realities and worlds, and safely communicate with other magickal adepts.

Waxing Moon: Place Eihwaz in any house where you need to repel danger, theft, and destructive energies. Use it to protect yourself, someone you care about, or anything else from dangerous forces.

Waning Moon: Eihwaz, placed within the Zodiac Houses of Libra #7 (Open Enemies) and Pisces #12 (Hidden Enemies), will banish any ill wishers, while diminishing their power against you.

16. Sowilo

Sowulo, Sigel
Sound Value: S

The Rune of: The magickal will.

Key Concepts: Defense and victory over oppressors.

Mundane Meanings: Sun or the Solar Chariot or Wheel.

General Meanings: One of the best victory Runes one could possibly use in any situation to assure success. Opposition of any kind to this Rune is quickly, effectively, and permanently dispatched.

Sowilo generates and places unlimited power at one's disposal to create changes as desired.

This Rune favors minorities, women, and anyone suffering from oppression or tyranny. It promotes prosperity, warmth, growth, and comfort in labor; victory over enemies is assured.

Health, power and physical strength, clear thinking, self-esteem, and self-confidence are part of this Rune's province.

Magickal Use: The ecstasy of communing within the light of the Sun Goddess Sol or Sunna. The Sword of the Flaming Goddess; it cleanses, heals, teaches, protects, and dispenses justice and retribution.

The Wheel of Light or the Sun, as this Rune depicts, is also related to the chakras (Spinning Wheels or Vortexes) within our bodies. It is by bringing down Sol into the body, through the crown chakra, that the ecstasy of union is felt. It is this power that opens, cleanses, and begins the progression of the serious magickal practitioner. Without the power of Sol entering into the chakra system, real magickal growth is impossible.

Waxing Moon: Place this Rune within any zodiac house where you require protection and victory, or to control and overcome oppression of any kind.

Waning Moon: Sowilo placed within any zodiac house upon the waning moon removes, exposes, and/or destroys hypocrisy, prejudice, tyranny, and oppression. Add Tir (Victorious Warrior) to Sowilo for strength and to correct any slight of justice.

17. Tir

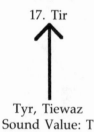

Tyr, Tiewaz
Sound Value: T

The Rune of: Victorious warriors.

Key Concepts: The Warrior or the Giver of Law and Dispenser of Justice.

Mundane Meanings: The God Ty'r.

General Meanings: Aggressive male energy; glory and good fortune; devoted peers. Instills loyalty, reliability, steadiness, guidance, self-sacrifice, and unselfish concern for others.

World order, justice, law, and spiritual discipline. Victory through conflict or struggle. The belief that the just will prevail, or might makes right.

Magickal Use: Faith through experiencing the elemental forces of magick and religion as one; Ritual Magick. To experience the truth and light for one's self. Spiritual battles within.

Waxing Moon: Be victorious, overcome, or block an opponent in battles, conflicts, court cases, and competitions. Tir can be effectively utilized in any zodiac house.

Waning Moon: Calm, negate, or diminish your opponent's abilities in any battle, conflict, court case, or competition.

18. Beorc

Berkano, Berkana,
Sound Value: B

The Rune of: The Great and Protective Mother Goddess.

Key Concepts: The Earth Mother; growth, containment, and concealment.

Mundane Meanings: Birch.

General Meanings: Beorc is ideal for sending energy outside of yourself to another person, place, or thing. It governs dwellings and all sacred areas such as groves of trees and natural sites (temples) of worship.

Fortune and happiness. All matters requiring secrecy and cloaking: love affairs, passion, and all matters of the heart. Fertility, babies, pets, and children; home life and relationships, all domestic affairs. Healings, particularly of a critical nature, either physical or emotional.

Magickal Use: To send through the use of Talisman Magick peace, fertility, protection, harmony, and love.

Within this Rune are the concepts of the life cycles or rites of passage: rebirth, puberty, motherhood, fatherhood, old age, and death.

Use Beorc to discover the magickal mysteries of the Maiden, Mother and Crone, and to work the magickal path of the Goddess.

In the use of Earth Magick, Shamanism, and Animal Spirit Helpers, this Rune protects and hides or conceals.

Waxing Moon: Build a strong healthy and vibrant family life. Hide an affair or bring back an errant lover. This Rune can also be used to call a desired lover to you that had previously not noticed you.

Waning Moon: Expose a love affair; banish or destroy disease;

break up any relationships that no longer serve your best interest.

Use with Gemini #3 (Good Communications), Cancer #4 (Home and Family), Leo #5 (Children and Romance), and Libra #7 (Spouse and Marriage).

19. Ehwaz

Ehwaz, Eh
Sound Value: E

The Rune of: Aggressive and quick changes.

Key Concepts: Movement.

Mundane Meanings: Horse.

General Meanings: Wherever this rune is placed, it brings about change (normally used for an existing condition) and usually requires travel of some sort. It is best used in conjunction with other runes that specify the types of changes that are desired. Use caution, as Ehwaz has a tendency toward rapid and reckless change unless specified otherwise.

All modes of transportation, travel or shipping. To create something new. Teaches trust, loyalty, dependability, and learning to work in harmony with others.

Magickal Use: The horse is a magickal animal and, for that reason, is frequently seen as a totem animal. It represents wisdom, protection, power, loyalty, reliability, and swiftness. Many ancient peoples (such as the Germanic races) mentally rode their horses when exploring new worlds, dimensions, or the inner realms of self.

The horse, being a form of divine protection, aided the traveler in his or her magickal endeavors. This is the ideal Rune for those with an affinity to horses.

This Rune is also used by men and women in rites of fertility (stud-insemination), and offers great peace, joy, and sensuality.

Governs all means or modes of magickal travel: astral, mental, soul, emotional, and projection.

After you have chosen the zodiac house in which you will be working, place your runescript (types of changes you want) within your chosen house. Now add Ehwaz to create those changes swiftly and as you have specified.

Waxing Moon: Add Ehwaz to any set of Runes (within your chosen zodiac house) where time is of the essence.

Waning Moon: When traveling, use Ehwaz to banish all obstacles or hazards that may hinder your safe progress.

20. Mannaz

Man, Mann
Sound Value: M

The Rune of: Humanity.

Key Concepts: The Magickan or Enlightened Ones.

Mundane Meanings: Homo sapiens.

General Meanings: To obtain the aid of others. Ego, self-knowledge, and inner learning. Cleverness, good will, mental and physical agility. The crafts person, the laborer; the Rune of the Magickan.

To manipulate or control intelligence, slyness power, and energy to one's own desires. Controlling the mental processes of self or others.

Magickal Use: "Initiate Know Thyself." This seemingly innocuous statement is the key, in fact, to immortality, wisdom, truth, and magick.

Mannaz aids in discovering the power of self or the God or Goddess Self.

It also aids in the union and melding of the three selves, hidden within each of us, that are responsible for creating the reality we perceive in our lives.

Waxing Moon: To place a thought into the mind of another, use Mannaz on a waxing moon. As outlined within this text, place all essential data regarding your target individual within the zodiac house of your choice. Next wrap or place your runescript atop this information. Each night at the same time, and while the individual sleeps, project whatever you wish into the mind of the targeted individual.

Also use Mannaz on the waxing moon to block all thought projections from others. Place the names and essential information of those you suspect may be projecting to you within applicable zodiac houses (usually under enemies, if not related to you or not a boss). Now block their energy by wrapping their information within parchment where Mannaz has been inscribed.

Waning Moon: To render any thought projections, controls, or others impotent, and to banish the manipulative or controlling energies of others, do the same as outlined above. The only difference is you are using Mannaz on the waning moon.

21. Laguz

Laguz, Lagu,
Sound Value: L

The Rune of: Transmutation and initiation.
Key Concepts: Water; to flow.
Mundane Meanings: Water, lake, sea, or liquid.
General Meanings: A Rune of aggressive female energy. From the sea all life manifests the eternal female and the regeneration of life.

Vitality, health, nurturing, cleansing, and the act of giving birth; the life force, especially for women. A very protective Rune for women and children; all matters dealing with feelings, emotions, love, and domestic life.

A Rune of the artist, arts, or artistic endeavor. All matters dealing with the sea; her dead, her treasures and secrets.
Magickal Use: Use in conjunction with Holy Water in magick and all rites of passage from birth to crossing over the black Void or Abyss. The Void or Abyss was also seen as a sea or lake that had

to be traveled by boat to reach the Summer Land, where one awaited a chance for rebirth.

All matters of a psychic nature or requiring psychic abilities, visualization, and intuition; dreams, prophecies, Women's Mysteries, the unknown, riddles, and the underworld. Secrets from the world of the Undines and the use of water in magick.

As an example of how Laguz and water can be used in combination as a talisman, the following is offered: *For Children Who See Spooky Things in the Dark:*

To protect any area from natural or unnatural forces (particularly for children's rooms), obtain a clear plastic spray bottle and fill it with spring, sea or "Holy Water." Inscribe the runic symbol of Laguz upon the bottle and energize or "charge" the fluid. Now use as indicated below for the waxing and waning moon.

Waxing Moon: To build protection within an area, spray the Laguz formula in a clockwise manner throughout your home, office, child's room, or any area where you find it necessary. This process will close off any rips, tears, or access points through which destructive energies can enter.

Take several photos of the area you are going to spray (seal off) and place your rune script on the back of each photo. Place a single picture within each of your chosen zodiac houses as suggested here.

1. Place Thurisaz (Defense) and Eolh (Victory Over Enemies) within Leo #5 (Children) to represent your child.

2. Place Beorc (Powerful Goddess-Motherly Protection Within the Home) in Cancer #4 (represents the targeted area or your home).

3. Place Lagaz (to take control of the situation), in Scorpio #8 (Occult Secrets, Other Worlds, and Discarnates [Ghosts]).

4. Place Eihwaz (Banishing) and Wunjo (Happy Endings) within Pisces #12 (The Unknown and Hidden Enemies).

By following these examples, you will have created a talisman that projects strong protective and parental protection to your offspring. You have taken control of the situation and banished any energies that might cause your child discomfort.

Here is one last item that is most effective that your child can use personally. Take the Energized Water that you formerly used to cleanse the area and place it within a squirt gun, or spray bottle.

Give the item to your children and tell them that whenever they see a ghost, goblin, or anything else that goes bump in the night, to squirt it. This has several positive aspects for your child. It teaches them that they are not helpless, and can take control of their surroundings. And, the Energized or Holy Water does indeed banish such undesirable creatures.

This total process sets up a highly effective Talismanic Shield of Protection for you and your family that can be renewed on each New Moon (Dark of the Moon) or as needed.

Waning Moon: Use the same method as outlined above for the waning moon. Only this time direct your Rune script to banish instead of protect. It is unwise to use a Rune for protection on a waning moon as you will undo all your previous work from the waxing moon.

In effect, what you are doing on the waning moon is releasing, banishing, and pushing away anything undesirable within the area.

22. Ingwaz

Inguz, Ing,
Sound Value: Ng

The Rune of: Binding.

Key Concepts: Fertility, male energy, consort to the Earth Mother.

Mundane Meanings: The God Ing.

General Meanings: This Rune fixes, holds, and binds your desired outcome in any situation. It also prevents all that you have worked for from slipping away, or being stolen by others, and, finally, prevents your Runescript or magickal endeavors from losing their potency. For these reasons, Ingwaz is a good Rune to use in conjunction with other Runes, especially just after Wunjo (Happy Endings), as the very last Rune in your Runescript.

Magickal Use: This Rune carries within it one of the best kept secrets of Sex Magick, an unlimited power for those willing to learn how to tap into its resources and secrets.

It is also used to clear out old energies that are a hindrance to lives, auras, chakras, and realities. It allows for the programming of new experiences and an enhanced life.

Waxing Moon: Use Ingwaz to build fertility in a male or a female. Sexual appeal and overall attractiveness to the same or opposite sex can be greatly enhanced with Ingwaz.

Waning Moon: On the waning moon, Ingwaz can have the opposite effect. A lover will find you less appealing and the fertility of anyone will be greatly reduced or blocked altogether.

23. Dagaz

Dagaz, Daeg,
Sound Value: D

The Rune of: A new day.

Key Concepts: Today is the first day of the rest of your life. Make it count with Dagaz.

Mundane Meanings: Day.

General Meanings: To begin anew; to transform or alter to advantage; to break though all blocks and barriers; increases or decreases for the better; new resolutions and attitudes.

Dagaz turns around the destructive or depressing and promotes a constructive and happy outcome. It also aids in reevaluating a situation or a circumstance, thus leading to a better position for more competent viewing. It is the Rune of awakening, persuasion, and realization.

Magickal Use: Use Dagaz when seeking new answers, to old or magickal questions, through meditation, ritual, and creative visualization. This is best done during the daylight hours due to its affiliation to daylight.

Waxing Moon: Dagaz used on a waxing moon is ideal for sending your thoughts to another and having them believe the thoughts are their own. It is through this process that others can be made to see things your way. Simply inscribe Dagaz, along with any other appropriate Runescripts, on the reverse side of a picture, parchment, or your Zodiac Worksheet that contains the personal data of the individual you want to influence. Then place this within the corresponding zodiac house of the person you wish to influence.

Waning Moon: To reverse or turn around someone's opinions, beliefs, feelings, or court rulings, use Dagaz.

24. Othalaz

Othel, Ethel, Othilla
Sound Value: O

The Rune of: Heritage.

Key Concepts: The cultural and familial heritage and traits one is born into.

Mundane Meanings: Ancestral.

General Meanings: Ancestry, the elderly, inheritance, wills, family prosperity, estates, heritage, place of birth, traits, Karma, prejudice, bias, ethics, morals, narrow mindedness.

Magickal Use: To communicate with the dead while seeking wisdom and the secrets of the Crone. Healing magick for the elderly (either animals or humans). It is the guiding Rune to aid the dying to the realms of the Summerland, Heaven, or Nirvana.

Waxing Moon: To visit with a loved one that has passed over, do the following:

Write their essential information in the middle of your Zodiac Worksheet. If you have a picture of the departed, place it close by.

Next, place Othalaz inside the zodiac houses of your choice: Scorpio (Death-dream communications), Gemini (Communications-channeling), Aries (Physical Body-physical manifestation) or, try a combination of all three.

Finally, take an energized candle that will burn for at least three days. Inscribe the runic symbol of Othalaz upon the skin of the wax, and then place the candle in the center of the Zodiac Worksheet, if you can safely do so, or someplace near where no fire hazard exists.

The departed will come to you in a dream, through meditation, or by other means when you are open and willing to accept their company.

Signs to Watch For:

1. Feelings of a presence.
2. Shadows.
3. Things appearing or disappearing.
4. Voices or strange sounds.
5. Dreams of the individual.
6. Seeing them in meditation.
7. Times when you simply cannot stop thinking about them; they are frequently near you.

Waning Moon: Often, people become earthbound and cannot cross over. This is most often due to grieving relations that selfishly hold onto the departed, not realizing they are doing harm.

For that reason, it is best to help the departed find their way by creating a Zodiac Talisman just for them.

First, write down as much as you can about the individual, within the center of your Zodiac Worksheet.

Next, prepare an energized candle that must be capable burning for at least three days, and inscribe the departed's name and the runic script of Othalaz in the wax. (If you are using an agent encased within a glass housing, simply take a grease pen or glass marker and inscribe your information upon the glass casing itself.)

Place personal items, such as hair, picture, comb, or whatever else you might have that was directly associated with the individual, in the house of Scorpio (Death and Rebirth).

On a separate sheet of paper, write your goodbye statement. This is the time to make amends; it is not too late and the individual will witness what you express. Above all, you must release them and let them know it is okay to leave.

Light your candle and let it burn for three full days, or until it burns out on its own. Three days is usually how long it will take for the essence or spirit to part from the physical. During this transition period, the individual will be visiting loved ones and reliving portions of their corporal lives while witnessing what others felt and thought about them.

Visualize a stairway leading from the candle to the Summerland. You may even see others on the stairway waiting for the departed; this is a very good sign.

While looking at photographs of the departed, explain your feelings toward them and that you will miss them, but you release them and look forward to seeing them again. If necessary, explain what has happened, if you sense their questions. Feel free to converse with them but encourage them to move on. Once across, they will be permitted to visit you as often as is necessary for a healthy readjustment.

If the individual has died from the effects of a long-term illness, alcoholism, or drug addiction, their minds may be clouded and their thoughts may be jumbled. In such cases, you must be patient, as they will be trying to understand what has happened.

This is especially true for those individuals who have died quickly and unexpectedly, as in the case of automobile accident victims. The victims often do not understand that they are dead. They need someone to explain what has happened. Otherwise they become earthbound, which can result in a haunting.

Finally, once you have helped the departed person or animal to cross over, take your letter, along with the picture and whatever else you have incorporated into your talisman, and bury it. Plant a favorite tree, flower or bush of the departed over the talisman. This location becomes a sacred place (shrine) where you may visit with the departed. It is a much nicer, and more appropriate, place for visitation than any graveyard where only a shell or mound of ashes remain.

25. Wyrd

Karma, Wyrd, Wishing Stone

The Rune of: Karma.

Key Concepts: The Pure Energies of the Void and Chaos.

Mundane Meaning: The Unknowable.

General Meaning: The blank Rune, as with blank cards, are pure chaotic energy. They magnify and project energy. This energy can be controlled by placing other Runes close by. Karma, from an action or an omission, is created. We are in a never-ending cycle of creating lessons and experiences within our lives. Like Karma, this Rune is endlessly creating something.

The best position for Wyrd is at the beginning of any Rune-script, as this energy is at it most basic, its infancy. It is programmed by placing other Runes or cards close by. Wyrd will channel the power of anything that lies close. Relate this Rune to a crossroad junction. Each road leads to a different destination. Wyrd, used in conjunction with other Runes, guides what you are manifesting.

To further illustrate. Think of any blank Rune or playing card as the Joker or wild card. While this is a fantastic Rune or card for creating havoc and chaos (due to its energy attempting to manifest in so many different directions), it is unpredictable and unruly.

This wild power, in most instances, must be harnessed by placing other appropriate Runes or cards along with it for directional control.

Magickal Use: Wyrd is a wonderful Rune whenever you are performing magick. It has tremendous power (being represented by pure Cosmic Energy-Chaos) and, for that reason, it is perfect in any magickal endeavor. Just be sure you are capable of honing and shaping this wild energy or your results will not be as you had hoped.

Wyrd is the Rune of the Joker, Prankster, or Coyote in American Shamanism. Should you unwittingly place four or five of these blank Runes within any given house you would create complete and total havoc and the results would be completely unpredictable.

To better explain this, when you use Wyrd, without the benefit of other runes to mold its wild energies, you are calling in karmic lessons of pure malleable energy.

So, do not think you are doing a friend a favor by stirring up their love life with a blank Rune. You would be calling in this person's karmic lessons (constructive and destructive).

Waxing Moon: Create or manifest anything new into your life. Wyrd is the rune of "As You Sow, So You Reap." Thus, for example, if you have someone sexually harassing you, create a talisman for this individual and place the blank Rune within the House of Leo.

This will bring forth all the karmic lessons the individual has earned that deal with the harassment of others. This is not destructive, negative, or black magick, as you have simply left it up to the Universe to judge this individual.

Another interesting way to use this rune is to place it in the appropriate Zodiac House of anyone who is corrupt or evil. The authorities will soon be on their trail.

Waning Moon: Wyrd is ideal for returning or dispersing destructive energy that has been sent to you either by mistake or a deliberate intent.

Be sure not to add any of your own ill feelings to your talisman when you create it, however. Simply allow the Rune to do all the work for you and justice will be more than served.

If you add any of your own ill wishes or feelings to the situation, no matter how justifiable, you set yourself up for a magickal backlash (karmic return).

Always let the Universe dispense your retaliatory or defensive magick for you and you will never be plagued by negative magickal karma. Nor will you be disappointed in the justice that will be served.

Chapter 9 Quiz

1. Fehu is used to create power. T-F
2. Raidho is the Rune of choice for safe travel. T-F
3. Perdho is not the best Rune to use for discovering the secrets of others. T-F
4. To bind two or more people for a single goal, use Gebo. T-F
5. To halt or freeze a situation, giving you time to re-think your next move, use Isa. T-F

Answers

1. True.
2. True.
3. False. All secrets are revealed with Perdhro.
4. True.
5. True.

PART FIVE

Playing Cards and the Tarot

10

Playing and Tarot Cards as Talismans

History: If you should ask anyone about the origins of cards, you will usually get vague answers, wild speculations, or unsupported theories. If you can uncover tangible facts for research, consider yourself extremely fortunate.

The search for the origin of cards, used for divination or amusement, can lead from an exploration of the history of Atlantis, to the ancient Chinese dynasties, or into the mysterious depths of ancient Egypt and India.

The Chinese of 1120 B.C.E. are believed by some reputable sources to have been quite familiar with, if not the originator of, the modern card's predecessor. The Imperial Library of Paris has on display several oblong cards of ancient Chinese origin that bear a striking resemblance to the Tarot cards of today.

There are many private collections of cards that point to origins in Asia, Africa, and the Mideast. In the hope of tracing the roots of various ancient card systems, words found on these cards have been dissected by scholars and occultists. The trails have led to no single discernible source.

The gypsies, a wandering Caucasian people believed to have their origins in India, and usually associated with fortune telling and mystery, are generally credited with the spreading of cryptic cards throughout the world. The enigmatic trail remains a source of speculation that adds to the luster and excitement of using these mystifying cards.

What is generally accepted by esoteric scholars is that the Tarot is a unique set of powerful images that affect the sub-

conscious mind in mysterious ways. These influences include the triggering of past life memories, insight into ancient forms of long-forgotten wisdom, the ability to foresee future and recall past events, and the ability to control destiny through the manipulation of channeled energy by using specific card patterns and symbols.

A further belief is that the ordinary deck of playing cards was derived from the Tarot. Keep in mind that it is the special combination of color, shape, and symbol that stimulates the subconscious to effect the desired, preplanned changes of the magickan. On this basis, ordinary playing cards can also be an effective and potent magickal tool for talisman construction.

Elements: Whether choosing to work with an ordinary deck of playing cards or with a favorite deck of Tarot, you will find that each "suit" of the ordinary cards, or of the Minor Arcana (Tarot), is related to one of the four elements: Earth, Air, Water or Fire.

As discussed in a previous chapter, the four elements are considered to be specific types of the Earth's "life forces." These "life forces" animate our world and are critical to the performance of any type of magick.

Found within the Tarot is a fifth element called either the "Ether" or the "Spirit." This element draws its energy from the Earth and the Universe, not from the elemental world. It is unique to the Major Arcana of the Tarot and is considered synonymous with the will of the magickan. While the ordinary playing cards and the Minor Arcana of the Tarot can control mundane affairs, the Major Arcana affects chance, fate, destiny, and karma. It works on a higher, more potent vibrational level.

We will first examine the playing cards and the Minor Arcana together, since they are so closely related. We will explore the Major Arcana at some length later in this chapter.

It should be noted here that by no means are these few pages meant to be the last word, or a major authoritative dissertation, on any one of these card divisions. On the contrary, this lesson is to be considered a quick and easy method of learning the root meanings of each card. There are some excellent texts that delve deeply into the full use and meaning of playing and Tarot cards.

It is these basic teachings that leads to the channeling of the deeper meanings and philosophies hidden within each card.

And with this profound understanding comes the equally important initiation into the inner realms of magickal power. We will touch on this subject also in the section devoted to the Major Arcana.

PLAYING CARDS AND THE MINOR ARCANA

The element of Earth (material world and needs), for instance, is most frequently depicted as a Diamond within an ordinary deck of playing cards; while in the Tarot, a pentagram, tree, plant, totem animal, soil, or anything that typifies the elemental forces of Earth is quite common.

To further illustrate how the concept of the elements are depicted, study the associations of each element on the next few pages. These associations will indicate in greater depth the relationships between the four elemental powers and the suits of the cards, along with how they might best be used to effect a specific outcome in talisman magick.

EARTH

Card Symbol: Diamonds or pentagrams, pomegranates, gnomes, wild animals, coins, disks, rings, and center-punched stones.

Representation: The material plane.

Lessons: Of wealth and the power money can bring. The fruits of labor. Status in business and commerce.

Concept: Female maturity, parenthood, and the fruits of life's labor.

Color: Rich earthen tones.

* Early mundane meaning: Merchants or businessmen.

Waxing Moon: To manifest material needs and attain goals in life.

Waning Moon: To banish negative energies, events, people, or obstacles that prevent material gain and/or success.

AIR

Card Symbol: Clubs or wands (**swords), staves, rods, batons, scepters, censers, and birds.

Relationships: Male, old age, death, wisdom.

Lessons: Dying, leadership, non-violence, wisdom, temperance, and youthful teachings.

Concept: Thought plane.

Color: Yellows and sky blues.

*Early Mundane Meaning: Peasants or paupers.

Waxing Moon: To build mental energy, power, knowledge, wisdom, and effect change through mind control.

Waning Moon: To dissipate undesirable energies, thought-forms, magick, and stress.

WATER

Card Symbol: Heart or cup, cauldrons, grails, water, and fish.

Relationships: Female, love, marriage, birth, childhood, pets, and children.

Lessons: The heart and family.

Concept: Emotional plane.

Colors: Blues and all shades of blue-green.

*Early Mundane Meaning: The early church.

Waxing Moon: Build love, emotional stability, psychic ability, and happiness.

Waning Moon: Releasing negative or destructive emotions, habits, fears, or beliefs.

FIRE

Card Symbol: Spades or swords (**wands), fire, salamanders, and athames.

Representations: Male, youth, the peak of physical power, power assertion (the attitude that might makes right).

Lessons: How to handle power, difficulties, and challenges.

Concept: Transmutational plane.

Colors: Oranges and reds.

*Early Mundane Meanings: The military.

Waxing Moon: Aggressive energy and power channeled toward some competition. To conquer over others or to achieve an edge over the competition.

Waning Moon: To diminish the edge others may have over you in some manner.

---

*The early French saw the four suits not in esoteric terms, but as exoteric or classes of people. This attribution was tolerated by the early church, where esoteric attributions were considered heretical.
**Some systems reverse swords and wands. Use the system that works best for you.

THE MOON

● ◑ ◐ ◯ ◯

Waxing

WAXING

In the attributes of each suit, the waxing and the waning phases of the moon are mentioned. The waxing phase is used for attracting or creating. The waning phase is used for the reverse; repelling or destroying. Remember, whatever is possible for a waxing moon, the opposite is possible on a waning moon.

WANING

Keep this concept of reversal in mind as you read through the card attributes on the upcoming pages and you will have absorbed a valuable key toward understanding both the positive or upright, and negative or reversed aspects of both the Playing and Tarot cards.

THE ATTRIBUTES OF THE CARDS

Instead of memorizing the often complicated and diverse meanings of seventy-eight cards, 156 if you include their reverse meanings, there is a simple, basic way to learn the root meanings of the cards.

As you become more proficient with this basic method, your subconscious will begin to subscribe new or additional attributes to your cards. Remember, this is how your subconscious communicates with you. It will guide you to whatever card is best for your talisman, at the time to do you the most good.

As you discern more and more in depth meanings from your cards, your definitions may differ slightly from someone else's interpretation of the same card. Do not be concerned if this occurs. In such cases, you, as well as the other person, are drawing upon a different set of life experiences, so naturally your basic understandings will vary.

As you study the following attributes, your subconscious will receive educational input that will allow it to develop naturally as you progress through this simple method. Soon, you will be able to pick up any card and know its root meaning by observing the elements, numbers, and symbols placed upon it.

A QUICK WAY TO LEARN THE CARDS

In a previous chapter on numerology, you learned the basic meanings of numbers. Now is the time to add that knowledge to what you have just read about the four elements. By combining this understanding and information, you will know the root meanings of fifty-two cards.

Hesitant? Doubtful? You will find out that you know much more than you suspect.

Here is a brief review of the numbers chart.

  0: Something is forming. The wild card.
  1: New beginnings, birth, success.
  2: Balance, harmony, unions, decisions.
  3: Production, children, creation.
  4: A solid foundation or a rut.
  5: Quick change or alteration.
  6: Home, work, family, management, stability.
  7: Spirituality, tests.
  8: Success, evaluation.
  9: Ending.
 10: From experience and expertise, a new cycle.
 11: Messenger (children).
 12: Driving force (teenagers).
 13: Creative force (adults).
 14: Mastering force (old age).

Remember this now? Okay! Now choose any number that you might like to create a talisman from. For this example, we will use the number 8, success.

Next, write down your chosen number on a piece of paper and the list the four elements just below it.

Number 8 Success

Earth

Air

Water

Fire

Now see if you can remember one or more of the key words attributed to each of the four elements along with the energies they govern.

Number 8 Success
Earth-money
Air-knowledge
Water-love
Fire-power

How did you do? Did you have to go back and look up the information? No problem. This information will soon become second nature to you.

Now let's see what we have created here.

Number	8 Success
Earth-money	8 of Diamonds/Pentacles
Air-knowledge	8 of Clubs/Wands
Water-love	8 of Hearts/Cups
Fire-power	8 of Spades/Swords

Are you beginning to see the pattern? Learning the root meanings of the cards is really just that easy. With this brief method, you can quickly ascertain the meanings of all cards. But how about the reverse meanings?

Remember the waxing and waning phases of the moon? It is by using one or more of the cards on a waxing moon that you create success in these areas.

By using the same card on a waning moon, you create a reverse situation. For example, assume that your goal is power over a situation at work. Your talisman will be created within Capricorn (remember the zodiac attributes?) to influence your boss. Place the 8 of Spades (power), the 8 of Clubs (wisdom) and the 8 of Diamonds (money) within Capricorn on a waning moon. Instead of the "success" of power, wisdom, and money brought about on the waxing moon, you have reversed the aspects to remove the mental block (8-Clubs) from your boss that was keeping you from a promotion and more power (8-Spades), and preventing you from earning more money (8-Diamonds).

In this example, you can add something that will tailor the action more specifically so you can be assured that the talisman is going to do exactly as you wish.

Just write down, on a piece of parchment the following: "I banish all influences that stand in my way of a promotion and I destroy any influences others may hold over [use boss's name here], which would keep me from this promotion."

There you are. You have just learned how to combine the meanings of numbers with the four elements to arrive at the root meanings of the Minor Arcana and playing cards. You have also seen an example of how to use the reverse meanings on a waning moon to arrive at a "positive" outcome.

By selecting any one of the other numbers listed from 1 through 14 and combining their meanings with the elements as was done with the number 8 in the example, you will have the root meaning of 104 cards.

There is one other item here that may have puzzled you. The example used a combination of cards to achieve the goal.

To determine which cards you might wish to combine is a simple task. By referring back to the numbers chart, simply combine the meanings of the various numbers (cards) that will add up to your goal. By using multiple cards, you are intensifying a single meaning.

Here is another example to clarify what you have just read: To create a love affair without commitments, attachments, or the complications of a relationship, select an Ace (1) of Clubs (mental), an Ace of Spades (physical) and three (from multiple decks) Aces of Hearts (mental and physical enjoyment) that you will place between the other two Aces in the zodiac sign of Leo (love). Your layout will be Heart, Club, Heart, Spade, Heart. This combination creates a comfortable situation without entanglements. Note also that there is a total of five cards. By reviewing the number 5, you can see that it is the number of change. This also indicates freedom. Thus you have created an open relationship for purely gratification purposes and, as desired, no strings.

Should you wish to create a situation that would lead to marriage, use one Ace from each suit of Clubs, Diamonds, and Spades, along with the three Aces of Hearts, which results in a total of six cards. Arrange the cards in the following order: Diamond, Heart, Club, Heart, Spade, Heart. The number 6 refers to home and family but also ensures that there will be physical, mental, and emotional love. Note that this time there is a Diamond placed in front of the Heart. This was done because, in our example, you wanted to marry for love, not money. The added Diamond here ensures that there will be enough money to live comfortably.

On the next few pages you will find each of the four elements and their numerological meanings laid out in greater depth and detail.

Diamonds - Pentacles
Matters of Money and Practicality

Zero - Joker - Wild Card

Waxing Moon: Bringing forth and incubating desired changes in money, business, and prosperity.

Waning Moon: Dissolve some situation regarding money before it has the opportunity to manifest.

One - Ace

Waxing Moon: To begin, create, or give birth to new projects dealing with opportunity and money.

Waning Moon: To dissipate anything that is blocking, hindering, or slowing new developments in wealth.

Two

Waxing Moon: To balance and harmonize money problems and pacify business partners.

Waning Moon: This card is best used for breaking free, dissolving, or pushing away from undesirable money partners, monetary ruts, entanglements, or stagnation.

Three

Waxing Moon: To produce money from one's labor, craftsmanship or ingenuity.

Waning Moon: Use to halt sales and production, while limiting craftsmanship and ingenuity. May also be used to dissolve or banish that which stands in the way of successful work.

Four

Waxing Moon: Creates a solid and comfortable financial base. Use caution here, though. Monetary slothfulness and stagnation can accompany this success. Use this card to build on, rather than to obtain a monetary goal. (Refer to the Eight.)

Waning Moon: Use to destroy stagnation and frail foundations from within. Good for getting rid of monetary corruption and old, out-dated political or social structures.

Five

Waxing Moon: Use to alter any monetary change quickly.

Waning Moon: Use for slowing or stopping any monetary situation presently under way.

Six

Waxing Moon: Use for a prosperous home, financial stability, and money commensurate with the job. A lower management or blue-collar card.

Waning Moon: If used under the waning moon, this card could severely handicap the financial stability of the home. It could create strife, hardship, and conflict due to stress.

Seven

Waxing Moon: This card is best equated with the obtaining of money through religious, scientific, medical, or other abstract, yet creative, means.

Waning Moon: Use here for the removal of the spiritual and religious stigma attached to money and its ownership. Will release money to a needy project that is held up by bureaucratic, medical, or scientific restrictions.

Eight

Waxing Moon: Use for monetary success and wealth building through shrewd organization, management, and business skills. A white-collar card.

Waning Moon: Use to dissipate or destroy the wealth or career field of another, or to reverse the attempts of someone attempting to destroy your wealth or career. It will banish all energies and obstacles that hinder your career progress.

Nine

Waxing Moon: Creates a shrewd but generous and honest ending to a monetary endeavor. Creates a "win—win" situation.

Waning Moon: Releases all negativity that would attract less than honest dealings.

Ten

Waxing Moon: Use for quick action, renewed strength, and new interest in old projects, business endeavors, and money matters. Enhances plans, thoughts, and schemes for future projects.

Waning Moon: Use here for slowing any renewed interest in old or existing projects, thus causing uncertainty, hesitation and discouragement. Dissolves support for future projects.

Eleven - Page (Tarot Only)

Waxing Moon: Receive news of new projects dealing with money, position, monetary vulnerability, and responsibility.

Waning Moon: Drains all support, enthusiasm, and energy from any new monetary project before it gets off the ground. Also removes monetary risks or vulnerability concerning new projects.

Twelve - Jack Knight

Waxing Moon: Promotes victory in all matters of money through determination and single-mindedness of purpose. Use to command another for money or to pay a debt.

Waning Moon: Drains away the energy of another. Removes foreign energies from the aura that drain strength, power, and energy. Inhibits bill collectors.

Thirteen - Queen

Waxing Moon: Promotes monetary abundance in all areas dealing with money and material comforts.

Waning Moon: Can reduce another to poverty. Sends away all that hinders your abundance.

Fourteen - King

Waxing Moon: Promotes the "Midas Touch." Wise and pioneering in the ways of prosperity, money, and business, this card creates wealth and attracts others of wealth to you.

Waning Moon: Places an adversary in a "jinxed" condition. A "Midas Touch" in reverse. Repels wealth. May also be used to dissolve destructive energies that would inhibit achievement of monetary goals.

Spades - Swords
Concern, Transmutation, the Physical World
and Body Power

Zero - Joker - Wild Card

Waxing Moon: Ideal for dealing with ailments within the aura that have not yet manifested in the physical body.

Waning Moon: Use to release and transmute the energies of disease.

One - Ace

Waxing Moon: Use to begin or manifest something physical into your life, such as a renewed body from physical exercise.

Waning Moon: Use to diet away fat, remove low self-esteem and depression

Two

Waxing Moon: Represents a physically active person that you may have a physical attraction for, an athletic teammate, friend, or comrade.

Waning Moon: Represents someone you aggressively dislike, an enemy or physical competitor.

Three

Waxing Moon: Represents groups, organizations, military units, political factions, or hierarchies.

Waning Moon: Represents competitions, wars, aggressions, and strife.

Four

Waxing Moon: Represents the foundation, roots or structure from which any group or organization is built. Use on a waxing moon to bolster and reinforce the whole.

Waning Moon: On a waning moon, this card creates havoc and destruction in a group or organization.

Five

Waxing Moon: Promotes quick and aggressive movement or progression, an offensive strike, or hostile takeover. This card indicates change through controlled aggression and conquest.

Waning Moon: Promotes chaos and decay in any group, hierarchy, or power structure as a necessary part of the life cycle.

Six

Waxing Moon: Represents home or office area, and those working or living closely within that environment.

Waning Moon: Breaks up any condition of boredom, stability and rut. Creates the opposite, i.e. chaos.

Seven

Waxing Moon: Promotes aggression and violence to physically induce fear to force others toward a particular religious dogma.

Waning Moon: Promotes non-aggressive action toward others in all matters of spirituality and religion. Harmonizes values and spirituality with Nature and those around you.

Eight

Waxing Moon: Promotes conquest; victory over others through physical action such as wars, competitions, and intimidations.

Waning Moon: Promotes loss, dishonor, and defeat through a lack of physical power.

Nine

Waxing Moon: Brings something to a physical and final conclusion. The finish line card. You may win the battle or competition but will have not have won the war or prize until all is concluded. Therefore, the 8 of Spades is ideal for winning but the 9 of Spades wraps up the loose ends for final victory.

Waning Moon: Prohibits the successful closing of a particular matter. Delays matters of law and gives you more time for action or defense.

Ten

Waxing Moon: As with all tens, it represents wisdom through experience; the result when new challenges are met. Enhances swift and accurate action, leadership, and respect.

Waning Moon: Represents a totally incompetent, disrespected individual who can do nothing right.

Eleven - Page (Tarot only)

Waxing Moon: When physical labor becomes too boring, as with the 6 of Spades, spice up your life with the Page. Promotes work enjoyment and popularity.

Waning Moon: Typifies the workaholic, or an individual that takes work too seriously and obtains little enjoyment from it.

Twelve - Jack - Knight

Waxing Moon: Represents an aggressive, honest individual who is basically a loner, or unsung hero or heroine, on a local level. Typifies a soldier, warrior, Amazon, police officer, or judge who upholds justice, peace keeping, and equality.

Waning Moon: On a waning moon, this card represents the totally opposite type of person. Usually typifies a dishonest politician, police officer, traitor, or criminal on a local level.

Thirteen - Queen

Waxing Moon: Indicates action tempered by conscience, experience and willful control. Represents fair State judges, State politicians, and high ranking military and police officers on a State level.

Waning Moon: Represents those who would corrupt, malign, destroy, incarcerate, or remove freedoms on a State level.

Fourteen - King

Waxing Moon: Wise and seasoned, the King of Spades represents the leaders of any nation in a field of physical endeavor, particularly those of the United Nations, National Guard, Armed Forces, and world class reformers.

Waning Moon: On a national scale, the King represents the dictators, oppressors, organized criminals, and world class terrorists.

Clubs - Wands
Matters of Wisdom and Folly

Zero - Joker - Wild Card

Waxing Moon: Use to plant a seed or idea by projection of your own thoughts and wishes. For communication and public relations.

Waning Moon: Use to weaken, return, or destroy the power of any psychic attack. May also be used to weaken the resistance of others to psychic communication.

One - Ace

Waxing Moon: This card guarantees success through communication via the media or public speaking.

Waning Moon: Use to break down barriers to effective communication with others when dealing with the public.

Two

Waxing Moon: Builds harmony in communicating with partners. A perfect card for negotiators and is powerful enough to use as a talisman for the swaying of opinion.

Waning Moon: Use to dissolve conflicts, blocks or differences of opinion held by those who oppose you and may hinder your success.

Three

Waxing Moon: Use to enhance success in all forms of communication where the final product is affected. The successful display of the fruits of labor.

Waning Moon: Use to destroy or dissolve anything that blocks or hinders your productivity and success. Thwarts the barriers to the "big chance" or opportunity.

Four

Waxing Moon: Use to build a solid and firm foundation from strong communication skills that will give you the edge over others.

Waning Moon: Use to banish insecurity, self-doubt.

Five

Waxing Moon: Develops miscommunication, confusion and disruption on all levels of communication. Most often used to create arguments or disagreements.

Waning Moon: Use here to clear away confusion and to reverse misunderstandings. Open a channel of communication.

Six

Waxing Moon: Enhances comfortable communications with employees, employers, family, friends, and relations.

Waning Moon: Use to banish all that would hinder your communications.

Seven

Waxing Moon: Use for successful communications dealing with the occult and spirituality. For channeling higher wisdom and running energy through the body for self-empowerment.

Waning Moon: Aids in the clearing away of stale, foreign or blocked energy that would hinder spiritual growth within the mental and auric body.

Eight

Waxing Moon: For success in all fields where the mind is essential. Enhances the will and therefore is popular with magickans.

Waning Moon: Diminishes the will and banishes the energy of others trying to dominate you.

Nine

Waxing Moon: Use to successfully complete a project dealing with any area of communication.

Waning Moon: Use to slow down, or bring to a complete halt, the success of others in communications. The cards thwarts the attempts of others who wish to harm your chances for success in any field of communication or science.

Ten

Waxing Moon: Use to quickly and successfully sway others by using any mode of communication.

Waning Moon: Use to diminish or halt the edge a competitor has.

Eleven - Page or Princess (Tarot only)

Waxing Moon: Use to create a quick and witty mind that will enhance popularity while having fun with communication.

Waning Moon: Use to banish those energies that hinder your own wit, charm, or charisma.

Twelve - Jack - Knight

Waxing Moon: Use to develop hard-hitting and aggressive dynamics in mental agility for the sciences, the performing arts, or any other area of communication.

Waning Moon: Use to slow or stop any hard-hitting, dynamic individual or group. Dissolves energies that hinder your own dynamic actions.

Thirteen - Queen

Waxing Moon: This card creates magnetism, popularity, charm, and charisma. It is perfect for celebrities, politicians, sales people, or anyone who wishes to draw others to them in a positive way.

Waning Moon: If your popularity, or the demands of others, becomes too intense, use this card on the waning moon to reduce your personal magnetism. May also be used to reduce the popularity of others, or it can clear away obstacles in your path to success.

Fourteen - King

Waxing Moon: Use to obtain the advice of others wiser than yourself. Aids in becoming an expert and to be considered so in areas of science and communication.

Waning Moon: Use to destroy mental blocks that can keep you from attaining mastery over any field of communication or science. It also renders ineffectual any attempts by others to deter your success.

Hearts - Cups
Matters of the Heart and Emotions

Zero - Joker - Wild Card

Waxing Moon: Use to create a lover whose identity is not yet known. Also for channeling universal energy to manifest the perfect mate, lover, friend, or companion.

Waning Moon: Banishes unknown energies and blocks that hinder your perfect mate, lover, friend, or companion from manifesting for you.

One - Ace

Waxing Moon: Draws a particular individual to you for romance, love, or an affair. Also useful for binding the love or heart of another, or planting the seeds of love, desire, or passion toward you.

Waning Moon: Use to make an individual lonely and more susceptible to your calling during the waxing moon.

Two

Waxing Moon: Will bring about engagements and marriage; also binds the love of close friends. Governs sexual unions.

Waning Moon: Enhances the chances for disagreements, separation, or divorce between couples. If the situation is already strained, it can reverse the conflict or situation.

Three

Waxing Moon: Can be used by an intrusive third party wishing to create a love triangle by stealing the love of another.

Waning Moon: Prevents the formation of a love triangle by diminishing the intruder's hold upon a spouse, lover or betrothed.

Four

Waxing Moon: Use to build a sound love relationship. This card can create a boring relationship, so use it with the Tarot Page/Princess to add fun to the relationship.

Waning Moon: When relationships no longer serve a constructive and mutually beneficent purpose, begin to let go by using this card. Soon the foundation of the relationship will dissolve and leave both parties free.

Five

Waxing Moon: Use to create a quick change in matters of love, relationships, or emotions where a situation is going stale or becoming boring, or if another person is stealing your love.

Waning Moon: Use here to slow down or halt existing changes in love or emotional relationships. If your spouse or lover is falling for another, use the 3 and 5 in the house of Leo. This will slow the action and begin a reversal.

Six

Waxing Moon: Use to create a happy and loving home, family, friends, and work environment.

Waning Moon: Use to banish existing unhappiness in your home or at your office.

Seven

Waxing Moon: Use this card to explore and experience the love of the Universe, God, or Goddess, and the Higher Self. Learn that the acts of love are beautiful and powerful when properly performed and can be used as a tool for energizing your talisman.

Waning Moon: Here the 7 of Hearts can destroy desires for love and create perversion, abstinence, impotency, and abuse.

Eight

Waxing Moon: Enhances happiness and success in all endeavors involving love, romance, and affairs. Can make you irresistible to others (a Romeo, gigolo, or idol).

Waning Moon: An excellent card for making a pesky self-proclaimed Don Juan lose interest. It works for both males and females quite nicely.

Nine

Waxing Moon: An ideal card for concluding a love relationship peacefully and parting as friends.

Waning Moon: Banishes negativity, boredom, and blocks that prevent a love relationship from reaching its full potential. Every relationship reaches a critical point approximately every seven years.

Ten

Waxing Moon: When a love relationship begins to wane, this card will quickly rekindle the fires of passion.

Waning Moon: Use here to blatantly end a relationship if that is the desire, but it will also banish energy deliberately or accidentally sent by another that might harm a relationship.

Eleven - Page or Princess (Tarot only)

Waxing Moon: Bring laughter and fun into an otherwise much too serious relationship with this card. This card also expedites all communications from loved ones that are separated by distance only.

Waning Moon: On the waning moon, this is the card of Cupid and, when used in a love talisman, sends or creates desires of love.

Twelve - Jack - Knight

Waxing Moon: When the one you love does not know that you exist, this aggressive card will clear the path to your intended. It illuminates the user by creating an aura of power and mystery that cannot be resisted.

Waning Moon: When the one you love loves another, weaken the hold of your competition with this card. Your competitor's attractiveness will wane, and you may then step in during the waxing moon.

Thirteen - Queen

Waxing Moon: The Queen assures abundance in all areas of romance, love, joy, and children.

Waning Moon: Banish all that keeps you from love and joy.

Fourteen - King

Waxing Moon: The King is the voice of experience in all matters of the heart. When in the need of aid or advice, or want to know the secret inner feelings of another, they will open up to you when the King is used in your talisman.

Waning Moon: When a loved one cannot open his or her heart and communicate inner secrets and feelings, the King responds on the waning moon. You become the King, a kind, reliable, and trustworthy figure for your lover to communicate with.

A PERSONAL VIEW OF THE TAROT TALISMAN

Perhaps you have seen the various images of the Major Arcana of the Tarot either inscribed upon jewelry, embossed on T-shirts, or drawn on posters. They are usually reproductions of one of the various Tarot decks in popular use, but the great majority are replicas of the images found on the cards that make up the Rider-Waite deck. This particular deck is very moving and quite powerful and is, therefore, one of my favorites for creating talismans.

As an experienced user of talismans and also having a high regard for the power within the cards, I purchased a Tarot T-shirt bearing the number 8 Major Arcana card, also known as the Tarot Card of Strength, as soon as I spotted it in an occult book store.

T-shirts with various Tarot symbols silk-screened upon them tie the individual wearing the shirt to the attributes and powers of the card and symbols represented.

As soon as I put on the #8 shirt, I energized the shirt and the symbols by calling upon the energies they represented. I now had a strength talisman with me wherever I wore the shirt.

The Major Arcana—as those of you who have used them as a tool of magick, meditation, and/or divination realize—predict periods of initiation within life. The word initiation in this case means a period of learning that can be painful or joyful, depending upon how this extension time is handled. One of the nicer attributes of the Tarot is that this initiation can be viewed in advance by attuning to the various card symbols.

Thus you can be aware of what energies are, or will be, at work in your life. You, therefore, know in advance what lessons you can expect to materialize.

In other words, being forewarned, you can become forearmed. In this way you can lessen any dramatic experiences and either avoid or alter other karmic lessons altogether. Remember, karmic lessons are not a punishment but are given as an opportunity to learn and grow. If a lesson can be equally learned by a less dramatic or painful means, then it makes sense to try to accomplish this feat.

A talisman can be constructed to aid us with any karmic lesson. Imagine lessening the effects of misery, sorrow, pain, poverty, and so forth. The power of the human body and mind is infinite. Combine this potential with the unlimited energy available to us from the Earth and the Universe and we can change the world.

Let us now return to the T-shirt I purchased. Approximately eight years ago, I began to go through a rough period of learning where my mental, physical, and creative stamina would be heavily tested.

To ease the burden and lessen the effects, I placed a Zodiac Worksheet upon a table top at home, and created a Zodiac Talisman that concentrated upon strengthening my physical body (Aries), my intellect (Gemini), my creative nature (Leo), and my outlook about those in power over me, my employer (Capricorn).

The cards that I placed within these areas on my Zodiac Worksheet changed almost daily at first, but the changing gradually slowed as I created a comfortable and manageable situation.

Ah, but what about my shirt? Well, I wore that shirt whenever I felt that I was under duress. And, by wearing the shirt, I had a direct link to the powerful talisman I had created at home, as the shirt had become an extension of the larger talisman.

It was amazing how well it worked. Had I no previous knowledge of magick, those eight years could very well have cost me my health and my sanity.

I could just as easily have used a silver necklace pendant or any other representation, such as the colorless Tarot cards, posters, rings, and bracelets that depicted the same #8 card, and it would have worked just as well.

The colorful posters are ideal for mentally merging into the card depicted and exploring the meanings of the symbols therein. You may be amazed at the deep understanding you can attain from such an experience for the creation of personalized talismans.

The black and white Tarot cards are similar to the posters but the merging is done as you apply the various colors to the symbols. The slow, careful application of color develops a deep, subconscious understanding more profound than a conscious merging.

In either case, the knowledge gained and the power developed from such work can only be really understood by those who have been initiated by the influence of each card. It is by working the various paths of enlightenment offered that hidden meanings and attributes are revealed to the serious seeker.

These hidden traits are revealed differently to each of us. Every card contains many abstracts and esoteric philosophical concepts found beneath the symbology depicted. Colors, numbers, letters, images, and the many combinations thereof, all create an intricate web. Each person gets only a small understanding of the myriad of symbols present in true Tarot cards.

This is a prime example of why there are so many different systems with numerous associations attributed to the various cards of Major Arcana. And why each card of the Major Arcana can only be loosely associated with a specific house of the zodiac. Each card does not contain the "pure" qualities necessary to be ascribed to a specific planet or house.

Therefore, to avoid confusion, think of the Major Arcana as being beyond normal methods of pure classification. They are, in fact, minute combinations of many associations. Scholarly occult experts have struggled to find the predominant and most obvious characteristics of each card. In this way, each card may be classified under one of the planets or zodiac houses for better comprehension.

What this all means to you is that each card holds, somewhere within its structure, hidden qualities of the planet or zodiac house to which it is assigned. Thus, the card may be used to represent that planet or house in any talisman construction.

As an example, under this mode of thinking, to represent the Goddess of Love, Venus, her sign, her vibration, or her signature as well as her attributes and characteristics, all that is needed is the Major Arcana card of the Empress (#3), even though the Empress has many other qualities that are obviously not attributed to the Goddess of Love, nor to the zodiac house containing the planet Venus.

As a further example of how this system might be applied, let me relate to you a short tale of how I applied the Tarot to another talisman.

As my desire to become a published author grew, I again called upon my knowledge of talismans to aid in this matter.

I began by purchasing a silver necklace pendant that depicted the card of the High Priestess. This I would later wear about my neck on a silver chain after I had energized it. I then laid out my Zodiac Worksheet on the table top and selected three other Tarot cards. They were the sun, the Star, and the Three of Pentacles. I placed all three of these cards, along with the pendant, into the House of Gemini and then energized my talisman.

To explain further, the High Priestess is ideal for enhancing the abilities of anyone in communications, i.e. writing. The Sun resonates to successful endeavors, the star to honors and recognition, and the Three of Pentacles to a finished work or product. Thus I had created my first talisman to become a published (Sun-success) and well-known (Star-recognition) writer. The products (Three of Pentacles-finished work) were my previous book, *The Candle Magick Workbook*, and this present one you are now reading.

As I create my correspondence courses, articles, my third book, and other writings, I faithfully wear the silver High Priestess pendant and keep the Zodiac Worksheet talisman within a picture frame next to my computer.

In the following section, the predominant attributes of the Major Arcana have been simplified into a few basic sentences. The listed traits are those found most helpful in talisman magick. They have been separated into waxing moon and waning moon sections so that the reverse powers of each card might be understood.

Any of the Major Arcana cards can be used constructively, in the upright position, on either the waxing or the waning moon.

For example, to create wealth, a talisman would normally be created on a waxing moon with the card in the upright position because all energies would be in harmony at the time for the manifestation of wealth.

However, if money problems are severe and time is a critical factor, the card may be used in the upright position on the waning moon to destroy, banish, or diminish any energies that are hindering the creation of wealth.

In the example, the same card was used to arrive at the same end, but in each case, the intent was what was different. Instead of creating, you were destroying in order to reach the same goal.

Since the foregoing is true, the reversed position of the card must also be effective on either phase of the moon. This is indeed the case, but caution must be used here.

A card used in the reversed position creates an opposite condition and emphasis is placed on all the opposite attributes of that particular card. The clue to successful use of the reversed aspect is again intent.

The Major Arcana

0 - The Fool - Uranus

Waxing Moon: Use to collect energy from the universe for the creation of any desired reality. To give life and form to that which as yet is only a thought, idea, or concept. Also used to coerce others into taking chances without the benefit of careful planning or forethought; the element of surprise.

Waning Room: Destroys the element of surprise and eliminates risk and excessive optimism derived from decisions made without forethought. Banishes the illusions that make things, situations, and people seem what they are not.

1 - The Magickan - Mercury

Waxing Moon: Enhances the potential for magickal or creative genius by ascribing the attributes of assertiveness, authoritativeness, inventiveness, and strength. This card also rules mischievous and cunning acts, organizational skills, and the power to persuade by oral or written means.

Waning Moon: Use to let go of undesirable traits such as rebelliousness, cowardliness, orneriness, stubbornness, and excessive assertiveness. Diminishes magical or creative talents.

2 - High Priestess - Moon

Waxing Moon: Enhances the gift of channeling wisdom and insight from higher sources. Governs the ability to effectively communicate information by any means. Calls forth latent magickal/psychic abilities.

Waning Moon: Aids in uncovering magickal charlatans, discovering the source of intrigue, and thwarts the magickal energies or endeavors of others. Hampers the ability to communicate.

3 - The Empress - Venus

Waxing Moon: Use to manifest abundance, love, joy, and pleasure in a creative but harmonious fashion within any aspect of life. A good card to use when attempting to influence or control social gatherings.

Waning Moon: Use to vanquish covert actions, attempts to prevent you from attaining happiness or abundance, by inhibiting negative or harmful energies.

4 - The Emperor - Aries

Waxing Moon: Use to create ambition, drive and motivation in yourself and others in order to attain a position of authority. Aids in the initial adjustment when you are promoted or become the employer, supervisor, patriarch, or protector.

Waning Moon: Dissolves the negative attributes of stubbornness, conservativeness, or the general misuse of power in the enforcement of social laws. This is also a good card to use for exposing those who misuse the power of office.

5 - The Hierophant - Taurus

Waxing Moon: Attain competency when dealing with social dysfunction, red tape, political corruption, and hostile or corrupt religious figures. Aids in the creation of new laws supporting honest social and political reform. Influences legal contracts, incarceration, institutions, or any other item or group that would restrict freedom. Teaching and learning.

Waning Moon: Use to expose political and religious corruption, social prejudice or any instance of "double standards." A talisman with this card in the reversed position on a waning moon is ideal for exposing and/or ending the career of a political figure. Such use would be very similar to a "curse."

6 - The Lovers - Gemini

Waxing Moon: Supports spiritual unions, soul twins, soul mates, karmic marriages, power through enlightenment, and the marriage of the Higher and Lower Selves.

Waning Moon: Use to clear away all that hinders or blocks you from experiencing your Higher Being and attaining your own spiritual perfection. Can be also used to make peace with the anima (female self) or anumus (male self), thus allowing you to find and experience your perfect mate.

7 - The Chariot - Cancer

Waxing Moon: Use to create calm from chaos, control the will, and to balance forces. This card also influences swift action, heroism, travel, ambition, war, strife, and the military establishment.

Waning Moon: Use to banish or weaken blocks, chaos, riots, quarrels, legal, military or political disputes, cowardice, and indecision. Lessens the danger and prevents unnecessary risk-taking in the performance of social, political, or military duties.

8 - Strength - Leo

Waxing Moon: Provides courage, inner strength, control, and confidence in one's own ability to achieve. Makes others feel weak, helpless, and insecure.

Waning Moon: Use to dissipate all feelings of insecurity, fear, self-consciousness, victimization and loss of control. Banishes discord and the negligent use of power.

9 - The Hermit - Virgo

Waxing Moon: Use to receive guidance, instruction, insight, or answers from divine sources. Undertake a vision quest for truth, wisdom, and spiritual development. Enhances desires to become a sage, philosopher, teacher, or guide in the aid of others who seek the path of spirituality. Influences for the control of any act of treason, rebellion, or hostile takeover.

Waning Moon: Remove obstacles or blocks that prevent enlightenment, sacred visions, truths, wisdom, or assistance to others along this spiritual path. Use to break down the resistance and forces of others who oppose your views, beliefs, or actions.

10 - Wheel of Fortune - Jupiter

Waxing Moon: Use to manipulate any circumstances beyond your conscious control such as karma, destiny, luck, or monetary problems. This is a good card for the gambler.

Waning Moon: Banishes energies that, when left unchecked, cause hopelessness, bad luck, misfortune, accidents, poverty, and sorrow.

11 - Justice - Libra

Waxing Moon: Use to call in karmic justice for any situation, or use to control any situation where justice may not be served. Covers the entire legal process. Good for partnerships.

Waning Moon: To use this card on a waning moon will ease the effects of any karmic dysfunction. This slowing down process allows time for regrouping and rethinking.

12 - The Hanged Man - Neptune

Waxing Moon: Use this card to bring any situation to a standstill. Create indecision, hesitation, and reasons to delay. This is also a vision quest card for use in a meditation talisman created to obtain wisdom.

Waning Moon: Use to break free of traits such as hesitation, indecision, and unnecessary self-sacrifice. Removes anything that stands in the way of receiving the necessary energy or knowledge to proceed.

13 - Death - Scorpio

Waxing Moon: The card of change. The old dies away (waning) so that the new make take its place (waxing). Create either a talisman of protection from mischievous earthbound spirits or a talisman of transcendence into the nether world to call down aid for lost or trapped souls.

Waning Moon: Use to release or transform the old and harmful energies of unhealthy habits, hurts, anger, and fear. Transforms destructive energies within your life into positive, life affirming energy. Banishes the specter of death.

14 - Temperance - Sagittarius

Waxing Moon: Use to moderate all matters within your life that are out of control. Learn additional control with regard to magick, diplomacy, timing, and habits. Balance the inner self with healing magick by controlling the energies from the Universe and the Earth.

Waning Moon: Use to release all imbalances and impurities within the aura, chakras, and emotions. Serves as an aid in releasing destructive forces that no longer serve a productive function in your life. Compassion.

15 - The Devil - Capricorn

Waxing Moon: Use to tie or bind someone or something. This is a powerful card for use in restraining others. Use it in talismans that require brute force, power, violence, and/or domination.

Waning Moon: Use to break free of restraining conditions or situations that enslave or bind you.

16 - The Towers - Mars

Waxing Moon: This card will create situations with sudden twists, turns, and changes. It is often used for influencing revolutions, wars, and other acts of violence such as retaliation, revenge, and anger.

Waning Moon: Use to destroy, alter, reverse, or shake up any violent situation. Causes chaos, thus providing for the needed change.

17 - The Star - Aquarius

Waxing Moon: Used for receiving spiritual enlightenment from Mother Earth or the Universe to enhance inner peace and serenity. This enlightenment invigorates, revitalizes, and protects, thus making the recipient a magnet for drawing in not only success, but the best of the successful.

Waning Moon: Releases all that taints, blocks, or is in any way inharmonious within the body and the aura. Prevents the blockage of enlightenment. A vision quest card that is excellent for meditation.

18 - The Moon - Pisces

Waxing Moon: This is a powerful card that can be used in magick for creating confusion, uncertainty, and illusion. It can literally overload an individual or situation, thus causing complete bafflement. It is the card of psychic and magickal abilities. It is best used to increase the magickal power of any talisman.

Waning Moon: Use to see through or break through the illusions of magickal acts of others. Rid yourself of mental or emotional turmoil and anguish. Use to thwart psychic warfare and vengeful magick. It is the card of choice for banishing psychic vampires.

19 - The Sun - Sun

Waxing Moon: The card of success, freedom, travel, honor, recognition, and goals achieved; a new start.

Waning Moon: Use to banish all that stands in the way of your success, freedom, honor, recognition, goals, or a new start. It crumples the over-inflated ego and destroys pessimistic attitudes.

20 - Judgment - Pluto

Waxing Moon: A card for winning in all areas but especially where the law is concerned. The card of regeneration; rebirth from changes made, renewal after a difficult time, and recovering from illness. Aids in the acceptance of your frailties, faults, and flaws.

Waning Moon: Dissolves destructive energies that permeate or surround the physical, mental, or emotional body. Releases all that creates illness or promotes self-destruction. Use this card to release energy cords that others have attached to your aura and chakras.

21 - The World - Saturn

Waxing Moon: The card of ultimate achievement. Your dreams and goals can come true. Attain mastery by seeing through the eyes of the adept in all matters.

Waning Moon: Use to banish all that stands in the way of achieving goals, dreams, or mastery in any chosen field of endeavor.

SOME FURTHER EXAMPLES

To further illustrate how the cards of the Major Arcana might be used in conjunction with the Zodiac Worksheet when creating a talisman, the Fool and the Tower cards will be used to demonstrate how each card is read and can then lead to a subsequent card for inclusion in the talisman.

Main Card: The Fool, used on a waning moon to create the element of surprise.

Second Card: The Tower, used on a waning moon to completely destroy the hold of another over a person or situation.

The combining of these cards intends that they surprise and destroy corrupted or negative influences pertaining to each house. Placed in Aries (physical), they could be used to overcome bullies; in Taurus, money scams; in Gemini, to thwart slick sales people; in Cancer, scams directed toward the elderly; in Leo, scams directed toward children, women, and sex; in Virgo, health and employment scams; in Libra, marriage scams; in Scorpio, insurance, tax, or death scams; in Sagittarius, religious scams; in Capricorn, political and law enforcement scams; in Aquarius, scams of friends or fraternal groups; and in Pisces, corruption within jails and hospitals.

Pregnancy: Should you wish to receive news that you are pregnant, place the Empress (fertility), the Ace of Cups (birth), the Page of Cups (messenger or child), and the 3 of cups (product of love) all into the house of Leo.

Success in the military, politics or law enforcement: To achieve this type of success, place the Emperor (the enforcer of law and social order), the Chariot (heroism), and the World (Dreams come true) all into the house of Aries.

Riches through gambling: Place the Sun (success), the Wheel of Fortune (good luck), the Ace of Pentacles (big monetary birth), and the Empress (abundance) all into the house of Leo.

Protection: For various types of protection, select the Chariot (power), the Emperor (protector), and the Sun (success). What type of protection you desire determines the zodiac house to use, i.e., Physical, use Aries; Money, use Taurus; or Mental, use Gemini.

Chapter 10 Quiz
Playing Cards

1. Zero, the Joker and the Wild Card all have the same meaning, according to this book. T-F
2. Eights are best used for success. T-F
3. Threes are ideal for those producing and selling their own work. T-F
4. Fives would create stagnation wherever they are placed. T-F
5. Tens mean success. T-F

Answers

1. True.
2. True.
3. True.
4. False. Fives mean change wherever they are placed; unless they are used on a waning moon, which would reverse their meaning to one of stagnation.
5. True.

Chapter 10 Quiz
Tarot Cards

What effect, if any, do the following Tarot cards have when placed in a given zodiac house:
1. The High Priestess in Gemini?
2. The Tower card in Scorpio?
3. The Lovers in Leo?
4. The Star in Taurus?
5. Strength in Pisces?

Answers

1. A talent for communication.
2. An unexpected or quick change with any matter regarding taxes, death, inheritance, gifts, or a partner's income.
3. Very effective for all manner of love talismans.
4. Success in some manner regarding money and business.
5. The ability to overcome any obstacles, hidden enemy, or incarcerations.

PART SIX

Appendices

Appendix A

MANIFESTING AGENTS

The Zodiac Worksheet is designed to incorporate, in the exact center, an object that will serve as a point of focus for the magickan's energy, serve as a transmitter for the combined output of energy from the talisman, and function as a receiver for any Earth or Universal energies that might be called into the talisman.

On the following pages, two such objects, the Wishing Stone and the Candle, are explained. Other agents may be used, as the type of catalyst is limited only by the imagination of the magickan.

As a conductor of energy and as a storage battery for the energy, the agent is ideal for guiding the talisman in the performance of its designed intent.

This is a handy little secret to know, especially when personal emotions might interfere or when unexpected emergencies might occur that would place a drain on the magickan. In such circumstances, whether a novice or an "old hand" is creating the talisman, the agent is the perfect answer.

After the talisman has been created, the next step is to energize the talisman and the object selected to act as the catalytic agent. But before we go into that phase, let's discuss the Wishing Stone.

WISHING STONES

Wishing Stones, like candles, have been around since the dawn of recorded history. Early man found various objects that, when rubbed between the palms or carried upon the person, seemed to enhance the luck of the owner.

There are a large variety of so-called wishing stones available today. The synthetic crystal, plastic, and metallic varieties are mere trinkets designed to amuse the user and to enhance the purses of the maker. They are found in variety stores and occult shops, and some may even be purchased by mail order. Beware of these trinkets, as they are rarely made of materials that emit the correct vibrations for energizing and manifestation.

A true wishing stone is usually made of natural stone, ideally quartz crystal, whose vibration enhances rather than detracts from the energy of the user.

WISHING STONES - A FORM OF TALISMAN

Wishing Stones are a form of talisman. A talisman is defined as anything natural or created that has been altered in some way from its natural or raw state and then energized by thought, desire, or wish.

As an example, a Wishing Stone made of quartz crystal is first altered from its natural state by cutting and polishing. This alteration is beneficial to the magickan as the design and cut of the crystal is intended to enhance its natural power. The crystal is then energized by the magickan to conform to his desire and will and to perform a manifestation.

THE CRYSTAL AS AGENT

The natural universe disperses esoteric wisdom to Channels and Magickans who are attuned to receive it. Usually these Channels and Magickans are people who have learned to tune in to the vibrations of the universe. They act like radio receivers, in a sense, and use the vibrational aspects of the crystal to amplify those vibrations. The crystal also acts like a transmitter, sending out energies that are intended to manifest a desire of the Channel or Magickan.

All people have the ability to send and receive vibrational energy. Most are not aware of this fact and that is why the terms Channel and Magickan are used to denote someone who has spent long hours learning just how to communicate with the universe.

To further demonstrate the ability all people have to transmit and receive information, it must be understood that our bodies are made up of tiny cells that contain liquid crystals.

These little crystals appear to act as miniature radios that receive and transmit information to and from the world and the universe around us. (This is why ESP is normal, not paranormal).

A Soviet scientist by the name of Dr. Alexander Dubrov performed 5,000 different experiments on living cells with the intention of discerning the truth about cell communication. His findings were proof that our cells do communicate.

It was by placing two cells into two different containers and joining them only with natural crystal glass that Dr. Dubrov discovered that the tiny cells emitted photons (particles of light or light waves called bioluminescence/energy) and simultaneously gave off ultrasonic radiations (sound wave communication).

When one cell was deliberately injured by trauma or disease, the other healthy cell, joined only to its companion by the natural crystal glass, somehow received the information from the first cell and it, too, died.

It was theorized that this information was carried to the healthy cell by light energy waves (vibrational energy) that were transmitted from the injured cell (similar to radio transmitting and receiving) and enhanced by the natural crystal in place between the cells.

In order to prove that the crystal enhanced the vibrational energy transmitted and received, Dr. Dubrov replaced the natural crystal glass with common man-made glass. Not to his surprise, the healthy cell and the injured cell could not communicate and no change was observed in the healthy cell.

According to Dr. C. Hill in his text entitled *Energy, Matter and Form*, "Like fluids in our cells, quartz is a crystalline structure." To a student of the occult, a quartz crystal Wishing Stone can become an amplifier of vibrational thoughts such as brain waves, emotions, etc. Thus, energizing a Wishing Stone is merely the act of transmitting one's own vibrational energy into the Wishing Stone, which acts as an amplifier and then transmits that energy to the universe for manifestation.

TYPES AND SHAPES OF WISHING STONES

As previously stated, each and every person has the ability to channel. However, the quality of either the transmitted desires or the received knowledge depends on several factors.

The prospective channel must first hone the ability to concentrate the thought patterns of the mind. This is accomplished by perfecting any of several mind control techniques such as Creative Visualization, Self-Hypnosis, or Transcendental Meditation.

Secondly, a link or amplifier of vibrational energy must be utilized; in this case we are discussing the Wishing Stone, but some channels prefer a candle, Tarot Cards, or other form of catalyst, in order to focus the transmitted or received energies.

The qualities of the material making up the stone as well as the shape of the stone are very important. This is why we have previously stated that many so-called wishing Stones are fabricated by artists or entrepreneurs out of various low-vibrational, natural or man-made materials as objects of great beauty but do little to enhance the energies of the magickan. They, after much time is spent in frustration in trying to make them effective, are relegated to the status of amusement pieces.

The most common and successful Wishing Stones have been created from various types of silica or quartz crystals, due to their special ability to amplify, store, and generate vibrational energy. Man-made crystals soon fail as their memories and energies wane, so the natural crystal is preferred. Clay, composed of minute silica crystals, may also be used when shaped correctly.

The shape of the natural crystal, when used as a Wishing Stone, should either be of a highly polished globe or semi-flat surface for omni-directional transmitting and receiving, or the pointed, multi-faceted shape of the natural quartz crystal for uni-directional activity.

TYPES OF CRYSTALS

The most common type of crystal used as an all-purpose Wishing Stone is the clear Quartz Crystal. There are many other variations of the basic Quartz Crystal. The color and the use to which the crystal is put depends on the "Impurities" found in its makeup. In other words, various impurities change the color and vibration of the pure crystal and thus change the use to which the crystal is put. Some examples are: (1) Rose Quartz-Love Wishes. (2) Amethyst Quartz-Spiritual Transmutation Wishes. (3) Smoky Quartz-Wishes for enhancement of the learning ability. (4) Tourmaline Quartz—very rare and expensive—manifests energy on all planes of existence. It is the preferred stone of magickans that need protection and great energy at the same time. It is similar to (5) Rutile Quartz—filled with tiny gold or silver fibers; this stone is jampacked with energy. It is widely used in magick to magnify the will of the magickan. It is excellent when used as a Wishing Stone and is generally preferred over the more common plain Quartz Crystal. It is also very expensive and difficult to obtain.

PROTECTING YOUR WISHING STONE

A Wishing Stone should never be carried exposed in a pocket or purse. Items therein could chip, scar, or injure it. The stone should always be protected by a soft cloth, leather, or chamois bag or kept in a box lined with felt or some other non-abrasive material.

Further, the stone is a private stone. It and its properties are designed for your use alone. It should never be fondled by another person and never, repeat, never, should be used for magick or any energy transmittal by anyone but the owner. The natural quartz Wishing Stone becomes attuned to its owner and can be damaged by foreign vibrations. Should anyone else handle the stone or should its energy become clogged, immersion in salt water overnight will cleanse it.

THE WISHING STONE AND CANDLE AS A CATALYST

After you have accumulated all of the materials for the style of talisman that you have chosen to make, and have laid out all the ingredients upon the zodiac worksheet, a properly charged Wishing Stone or candle, placed in the center of the Zodiac Worksheet, will focus and guide your energies out to the universe for manifestation or receive those energies that you have decided to call in. It is not absolutely necessary to add the power of a Wishing Stone or candle to your talisman; either the Wishing Stone, the candle, or the talisman will do perfectly well on its own, but an agent can be added as an enhancement to the power of the talisman.

THE CANDLE

The candle, as well as the Wishing Stone discussed earlier, is a vital catalyst for anyone who might need an extra boost of power for talisman magick or require a convenient point of focus when energizing the talisman.

The candle, whether in the ancient form of a wick placed in a bowl of tallow or some form of slow-burning oil, down to the modern beeswax or paraffin based tapers and votives, has been a part of magickal history since the first caveman used it to summon the spirits of totems.

It has been used by magickans, priests, shamans, rabbis, witch doctors, and the like to perform as a tool whose functions have been as diverse as a sole agent for magickal manifestation, a spiritual contact point, a divining tool, and, to our present use, as a catalyst for talisman magick.

In our book entitled *The Candle Magick Workbook*, also published by Citadel Press, candle attributes such as colors and associated scents are discussed in detail. If you wish to make a *very* powerful talisman, combine the candle magic technique found there with the talisman magick techniques found in this book. That is strictly up to you. For our purposes here, though, we will only discuss the effective use of a candle as one of the many agents that can be used.

ENERGIZING THE AGENT

The type of talisman that you are constructing and what your goals are will make a difference as to what sources you will use for energizing your agent and talisman.

Here are three basic sources for giving your agent and talisman the energy they need to complete their mission and to comply with your will:

Personal Energy: Personal energy is just what it sounds like. It is the energy you expend and place into any object. This can be done in a variety of ways, but the most prevalent is through concentration and visualization.

Begin by rubbing the agent gently between the palms of your hands, with the face of the agent touching your right palm and the back of the agent touching your left palm. If the agent is oblong, as in the case of a candle or some types of crystals, the right hand holds the top while the left hand holds the bottom.

As the agent warms to your caresses, concentrate your mind's energies on the goal you have in mind. Keep the picture of your goal very simple and very clear. Repeat aloud the purpose for which the talisman was created and the function the agent is to perform.

Stare intently at the talisman and the agent while visualizing in your mind beams of light energy. Feel the energy radiating throughout your body and exiting through the palms of your hands into the talisman and the agent, imbuing them with your will.

Do not be alarmed if your hands become hot. This is a very good sign that your energy is powerful. The heat is also an indication that you have been successful in your energizing attempt.

When you feel that you have sufficiently imbued your agent and talisman with your personal energy, place the agent into the center of the Zodiac worksheet and, in the case of a candle, light the candle.

Next, picture that energy (your goal) encased in a protective ball of light of whatever color seems right to you at the time. This ball of light protects the energy from others who may wish to thwart your goals by stealing or perverting that energy.

Now, let that ball of light, which contains your goal in the form of personal energy, out into the universe. See it float off, perfectly safe and protected, to manifest your goal.

Before you begin to congratulate yourself, there is one more function that must be performed. You must now re-energize yourself and remove any connections to the agent or talisman or you will drain back the energy from the talisman and the agent that you have just expended.

This is done by sitting, cross-legged if you are agile enough, on the floor and stretching out as far as you can comfortably do so. Place your palms flat against the floor. Close your eyes and envision all the remaining tension in your mind and body transforming into a healing color (whatever color feels right for you) and draining off into Mother Earth.

Next ask Her to exchange that energy for fresh, invigorating energy in a color that you need for self-healing. This exchange is a positive function and will benefit both you and Mother Earth.

EARTH AND UNIVERSAL ENERGY

The technique for using energy other than your own personal energy is basically the same, as illustrated above. Instead of summoning up the energy from within yourself, envision either colored light energy entering your feet from Mother Earth and then radiating throughout your body and into the objects through your palms, or envision colored Universal light energy beaming down through the top of your head into your body. As with personal energy, be sure to re-energize yourself afterwards.

By whatever method that you might choose to energize the talisman and the agent (if an agent is used), the main idea is to empower the creation to manifest your will. The agent is merely an additional tool to ensure success by drawing upon unseen energies and concentration either into or out from the talisman, something not all of us are normally capable of without aid.

What this means to the practitioner is that you do not have to be powerful or knowledgeable to tap into the energy sources necessary to create a powerful and potent talisman.

For those who find no problems in energizing a talisman without aid, the agent can also intensify the already strong magickal abilities in much the same way.

Appendix B

MAKING YOUR OWN TOOLS AND WORK AREA

The Talisman Table: The use of a circular wrought iron and wood table with an encircling lip about 1/2" high has proved to be the most often used table by students of Talisman Magick. A round sheet of glass or plastic placed over the finished talisman adds a nice touch.

The raised lip on the table affords sufficient clearance for any symbolic material, thicker than the playing or Tarot cards, used in the talisman construction. The circular glass cover can be made large enough to lie upon the lip so that the material below is untouched but is also protected from candle wax, wind, pets, and little fingers.

The nice thing also about using a covered table is that it can also be a useful piece of furniture that is not limited by its function as a talisman base.

Should you have selected a candle as your agent, simply place the candle into a base atop the tablecloth. Neither the glass nor the table cloth nor the candle, being "out of direct contact " with the Zodiac Worksheet, will effect your work in the least, and no one will suspect what is going on underneath.

The Talisman Picture: For some people, a low table is not always feasible. In that case, take your Zodiac Worksheet and place it in a glass-enclosed picture frame. You may then place the talisman construction material on the Zodiac Worksheet after removing the glass, and when the glass is replaced, it will hold the objects intact for placing the talisman upon a table or hanging it upon a wall.

An alternative method of using the glass picture frame is to seal the Zodiac Worksheet under the glass and then place a velcro strip on the outside of the glass. By placing other velcro strips on the backs of the talisman construction materials, you have created a talisman that is functional, decorative, and easily changed.

Appendix C

CHARTS AND GRAPHS

QUICK AND EASY TALISMAN USING THE I-CHING

	CH'IEN	TUI	LI	CHEN	SUN	K'AN	KEN	K'UN
CH'IEN ☰ GREATNESS	1 CH'IEN — UNIVERSAL ENERGY UNLIMITED POWER	10 LU — SECRETS OF SAFE CONDUCT REGARDING OTHERS	13 T'UNG JEN — SUCCESS THROUGH FRIENDS & ASSOCIATES	25 WU WANG — CATCH OR CAUGHT OFF GUARD & UNAWARE	44 KOU — TO TEMPT OR BE TEMPTED	6 SUNG — RESOLVING CONFLICTS & A CUNNING OPPOSITION LAWSUITS	33 TUN — THE JOURNEY WITHIN / FOR KNOWLEDGE & SECRETS	12 P'I — DECADENCE OVER COMES THE RIGHTIOUS & POWERFUL
TUI ☱ SENSUAL	43 KUAI — TO EXPOSE & REMOVE THE CORRUPT	58 TUI — FUFILLMENT PLEASURE ABUNDANCE GREAT JOY	49 KO — SURPRISE REVOLT OVER TURN QUICK CHANGE	17 SUI — THE SECRETS OF NATURE BRINGS SUCCESS	28 TA KUO — CREATE OR DRAIN -EXTRA ENERGY & POWER	47 K'UN — TO DEPLETE OR WEAKEN THE HONEST	31 HSIEN — TRUE LOVE YOUNG LOVE UNSELFISH LOVE	45 TS'U — TO BRING TOGETHER FOR A COMMON GOAL
LI ☲ INTUITION	14 TA YU — ABUNDANCE PROSPERITY & GOOD FORTUNE IN ALL THINGS	38 K'UEI — SQUABBLES FIGHTS & DISCORD	30 LI — SUCCESS THROUGH HUMANITARY EFFORTS	21 SHIH HO — TO SEND OR CALL IN KARMIC JUSTICE / TO MAKE RIGHT	50 TING — THE CAULDRON SECRETS OF EARTH MAGICK	64 WEI CHI — COMPLETE ANY MATTER	56 LU — WONDERER & THE PROBLEMS OF THE TRAVELER	35 CHIN — REWARD & RECOGNITION FOR EFFORT & WORK
CHEN ☳ RENEW	34 TA CHUAN — GREAT POWER, ENERGY & STRENGTH	54 KUEI MEI — SOCIAL OR ETHICAL VIOLATIONS BAD LUCK	55 FENG — ABUNDANCE AT ITS PEAK AND IN ALL AREAS OF LIFE	51 CHEN — TO CREATE OR PREVENT SHOCKING POWER & RESULTS	32 HENG — LIBERATION FREEDOM SOLVING A PROBLEM	40 CHIEH — TO RENEW LOVE A MATURE LOVE & STABILITY	62 HSIAO KUO — SMALL IRRITATING PROBLEMS THAT BIND	16 YU — JOINING MANY INTO A SINGLE & UNITED FORCE
SUN ☴ SUBTLE	9 HSIA CH'U — TAMING THE LARGER & MORE POWERFUL	61 CHUNG FU — POPULARITY FRIENDS RELATIONS	37 CHIA JEN — A HAPPY FAMILY GOOD FORTUNE3	42 I — BOSSES & THOSE OVER YOU ELECTED OFFICIALS	57 SUN — TO FOLLOW AS DIRECTED OBEY COMPLY & MIND	59 HUAN — TO BANISH OR DIMINISH ALL THAT HINDERS	53 CHIEN — SLOW & STEADY PROGRESS A HAPPY MARRAGE	20 KUAN — ABILITY TO ANALYSE & FORESEE FUTURE NEED/ACTION
K'AN ☵ DIFFICULTY	5 HSU — LEARNING PATIENCE & KNOWING WHEN TO TAKE ACTION	60 CHIEH — TO LIMIT REGULATE OR RESTRAIN	63 CHI CHI — THE EVENTS AFTER A SUCCESSFUL ENDEAVER	3 CHUN — TO SHORTEN DIFFICULTIES	48 CHING — TO GO WITHIN DISCOVERING THE POWER OF SELF	29 K'AN — TO CREATE OR BREAK BAD LUCK & DANGER	39 CHIEN — PERSONAL INJURY RESTRAINT IMPEDED PROGRESS	8 PI — TO UNITE MANY FOR A COMMON GOAL BRINGS LOYALTY
KEN ☶ MUTE	26 TA CH'U — VICTORY FOR THE STRONG & POWERFUL	41 SUN — SELF SACRAFICE LEADS TO DECREASE INCREASE	22 PI — ILLUSIONS MASKS BEAUTY TO ADORN	27 I — RENEWING & BALLANCING THE MAGICKAL SELF	18 KU — TO BUILD OR REPAIR QUICKLY --- TO PREVENT DECAY	4 MENG — CHAOS FOLLY CONFUSION	52 KEN — TO PAUSE TIME OR A PERIOD OF TIME OUT	23 PO — ADVERSE FORCES WEAKEN, ATTACK
K'UN ☷ POWERFUL	11 T'AI — BANISH MISFORTUNE SUCCESS & PROSPERITY ABOUND	19 LIN — TO DRAW GREAT FAME FORTUNE & SUCCESS TO YOU	36 MING I — OPPRESSION INJURY HARM DISHONESTY	24 FU — TO MAKE AMENDS --TO MAKE RIGHT OR CORRECT	46 SHENG — TO ADVANCE NEW PATHS GROWTH POTENTIAL	7 SHIH — A GREAT LEADER OF PEOPLE /ARMY REBELLION OR REFORMER	15 CH'IEN — TO ACHIEVE INNER & OUTER PROSPERITY & SUCCESS	2 K'UN — UNLIMITED SUCCESS & THE SECRETS OF MAGICK
↑ →	CH'IEN POWER ☰	TUI GREAT JOY ☱	LI BRILLIANT ☲	CHEN CHANGE ☳	SUN PENETRATE ☴	K'AN PERIL ☵	KEN STEADFAST ☶	K'UN WISDOM ☷

RUNES AT A GLANCE PART ONE		
SYMBOL	DISCRIPTION OF USE	KEY PHRASES
ᚠ	THE AVAILABILITY OF POWER FOR THE MANIFESTATION OF WEALTH AND PROSPERITY. USE TO EXPEDITE ANY MATTER, AND PROJECT YOUR WILL .	RAW POWER
ᚢ	THE ACT OF MANIFESTING. THIS RUNE AMPLIFIES THE WILL OF THE MAGICKAN AND CONTROLS OR MANIFESTS ANY DESIRES.	SHAPING RAW POWER WITH THE WILL
ᚦ	TO WIELD RAW POWER FROM THE UNIVERSE FOR MANIFESTATION, DEFENSE, DESTRUCTION OR WHENEVER YOU NEED THE EXTRA BOOST OF POWER FOR MANIFESTATION.	DIRECTING POWER BY SHEER FORCE OF THE WILL
ᚨ	CHANNELING THE OLD AND ANCIENT ONES. THIS IS THE RUNE OF MAGICK , EFFECTIVE COMMUNICATIONS AND MESSAGES . USE WHEN EVER YOU ARE SPEAKING	COMMUNICATION ON ALL LEVELS & IN ALL FORMS
ᚱ	TO JOURNEY OR TRAVEL BY ANY MEANS PHYSICAL, MENTAL OR ASTRAL. THE RUNE OF JUSTICE AND PARTICULARLY GOOD FOR COURT OR LEGAL CASES. IT IS THE RUNE FOR THE INNOCENT.	JUSTICE SERVED
ᚲ	THE CREATIVE FIRES OF LIFE AND PASSION, CONTROLLED BY THE WILL; CREATION; SEXUAL EXPRESSION; NEW REALITIES.	MAGICK & CREATIVE SELF EXPRESSION
ᚷ	A PERFECT BALANCE BETWEEN MALE AND FEMALE ENERGY, SEX MAGICK. FUNNELING ENERGY FROM TWO OR MORE TO CREATE GREAT POWER FOR A COMMON GOAL IN MAGICK.	PARTNERSHIPS, UNIONS, GROUPS , BALANCE & MARRIAGES
ᚹ	THE RUNE OF ULTIMATE JOY, HAPPINESS, ECSTASY AND PLEASURE. USE THIS RUNE IN ALL MAGICK TO ENSURE THAT YOUR MAGICK WILL BE SUCCESSFUL AND FULFILLING.	TO BRING A HAPPY ENDING TO ANY SITUATION
ᚾ	FOR SLOW AND STEADY PROGRESS NO MATTER HOW DIFFICULT THE OBSTACLE. BRINGS GOOD LUCK AND DISSOLVES ALL NEGATIVE INFLUENCES WHERE USED.	PROGRESS ACHIEVED.
ᛉ	A TIME FOR CLEANSING, BALANCING AND HARMONIZING WITHIN ONESELF. THIS RUNE BREAKS UP DISTRESSFUL SITUATIONS AND IS GOOD FOR FINDING TRUE LOVE.	DELIVERANCE FROM NEED AND DISTRESS
ᛁ	TO CREATE A STANDSTILL. TO BIND OR IMPEDE AS DESIRED AND FOR ONE'S OWN BENEFIT	TO FREEZE OR HALT
ᛜ	TO CREATE ABUNDANCE AND PLENTY IN ALL AREAS OF LIFE. GOOD FOR BRINGING IN MONEY THAT IS OWED AND BRINGS LUCK TO ALL LEGAL MATTERS CONCERNING MONEY.	REAPING THE REWARDS DUE YOU

RUNES AT A GLANCE PART TWO		
SYMBOL	DISCRIPTION OF USE	KEY PHRASES
	A POWERFUL RUNE FOR DEFENDING ONESELF OR ANOTHER WITH WISDOM, AND WITH THE INTENSITY OF LIFE AND DEATH ITSELF. A POWER, PROTECTION AND BANISHING RUNE.	TO VANQUISH PROTECT & BANISH
	TO REVEAL ALL THAT HAS BEEN HIDDEN OR OBSCURED. TO FIND OUT THE SECRETS OF OTHERS; TO LOCATE LOST OR STOLEN ITEMS, AND TO FIND BURIED TREASURE.	TO GAMBLE OR TAKE SOME RISK
	THE DEVINE SHIELD OF PROTECTION. IT CREATES VICTORY IN THE FACE OF IMPOSSIBLE ODDS AND CREATES LEGENDARY HEROES FOR THAT REASON.	DEVINE PROTECTION AND VICTORY
	DEFENSE AND VICTORY OVER THOSE WHO WOULD DO YOU AN INJUSTICE; OPPRESS, OR HARM. IT IS A GUIDING RUNE FOR THOSE SEEKING THEIR OWN PATH THE GOD/DESS.	THE MAGICAL WILL
	TO CALL DOWN DEVINE INTERVENTION , JUSTICE, OR KARMA UPON A SITUATION . THIS RUNE MAKES ONE POWERFUL AND GREAT AMONG THE MEN AND WOMEN.	POWER OF THE WARRIOR OR WARRIORESS
	THE EARTH MOTHER; FOR GROWTH; CONTAINMENT AND CONCEALMENT. FOR LEARNING THE SECRETS OF EARTH MAGICK AND PROTECTING THE HOME AND RITUAL AREA .	THE GREAT PROTECTIVE MOTHER
	FOR CREATING AGGRESSIVE AND QUICK CHANGES, MADE IN ACCORDANCE WITH THE WILL.	QUICK MOVEMENT OR CHANGE
	TO CALL DOWN THE ENLIGHTENED ONES AND CALL UP ON THE MAGICKIAN WITHIN ONESELF. PROTECTS THE ADVENTURESOME AND FACILITATES CHANGE.	HUMANITY
	TO RISE ABOVE, OR TRANSMUTE A GIVEN SITUATION OR PERSON. THE RUNE OF FEMALE POWER, THE AMAZON. TO CONTACT THE FEMALE POWER WITHIN ONESELF & MAGICK.	TRANSMUTE
	MALE FERTILITY AND ENERGY. THIS RUNE ENSURES A SUCCESSFUL ·MAGICK AND RELEASES ENERGY QUICKLY. THESUDDEN RELEASE OFTEN CATCHES OTHERS OFF GUARD.	TO BIND
	WHEN BAD MISTAKES HAVE BEEN MADE, & DOORS SEEMINGLY CLOSED TO YOU. THIS RUNE GIVES YOU A SECOND CHANCE; PROMOTES A CHANGE OF MIND & HEART.	A NEW START
	USE TO PROTECT YOUR WEALTH, PROPERTY. IT IS ALSO GOOD FOR PROTECTING AND HEALING ELDER FAMILY MEMBERS.	HERITAGE
	PLACE THIS RUNE WITHIN ANY TALESMAN OR SPELL TO PLANT THE SEEDS OF SOMETHING DYNAMIC, POWERFUL AND NEW. THIS RUNE REPRESENTS UN-MANIFESTED ENERGY/POWER.	KARMA , REBIRTH SOMETHING IS FORMING/COMING

Playing Cards and the Minor Arcana

NAME OF ZODIAC HOUSE AND THE RULING ELEMENT	DIAMONDS PENTACLES WEALTH EARTH / YEARS	CLUBS WANDS MENTAL AIR / MONTHS	HEARTS CUPS EMOTION WATER / DAYS	SPADES SWORDS ACTION FIRE / WEEKS	HOUSE MEANING AND RULING PLANET
1 ARIES FIRE / Aces	NEW JOB OFFER	A NEW OUTLOOK	A NEW LOVE INTEREST	A NEW SELF IMAGE & PHYSIC	I AM / MARS / BIRTH
2 TAURUS EARTH / Deuces	BUILDING WEALTH PROSPERITY & ABUNDANCE	BUILDING MENTAL AGILITY IN COMMERCE	BUILDING A LOVE RELATION FOR SOMEONE WITH MONEY	BUILDING A FORTUNE SWIFTLY & PHYSICALLY	I ACQUIRE / VENUS / BUILDER
3 GEMINI AIR / Treys	TO PRODUCE PROSPERITY THROUGH COMMUNICATION	TO PRODUCE COMMUNICATION THROUGH ESP & MENTAL AGILITY	TO PRODUCE COMMUNICATION THROUGH EMOTIONS/LOVE	TO PRODUCE COMMUNICATION THROUGH PHYSICAL ACTION	COMMUNICATE / MERCURY / PRODUCE
4 CANCER WATER / Fours	FOUNDATION OF FAMILY WEALTH & YOUR FEELINGS	FOUNDATION OF THE FAMILIES MENTAL OUTLOOK	FOUNDATION OF EMOTIONAL STABILITY OF THE FAMILY UNIT	FOUNDATION OF THE FAMILY BASED UPON THEIR ACTIONS	I PERCEIVE / MOON / FOUNDATION
5 LEO FIRE / Fives	A CHANGE IN MONEY, RISK, PROSTITUTION, CRAFTSMANSHIP	A CHANGE IN CREATIVITY, OUTLOOK & MENTAL THINKING	A CHANGE IN KIDS LOVE, MUSIC, FUN, SOCIAL ACTIVITIES	A CHANGE IN SEX, SPORTS, HOBBIES & COMPETITIONS	I EXPERIENCE / SUN / CHANGE
6 VIRGO EARTH / Sixes	RESPONSIBILITY & SERVICE IN FOOD, MONEY, HOME, & FAMILY	RESPONSIBILITY & SERVICE IN MENTAL HEALTH, THE LAW, GOVT.	RESPONSIBILITY & SERVICE IN FAMILY SERVICES & COUNSELING	RESPONSIBILITY & SERVICE IN REPAIRS, DOCTORS, SALES, TRAVEL AGT	I SERVE / MERCURY / RESPONSIBILITY
7 LIBRA AIR / Sevens	STABILIZES MONEY, PARTNERS, MATES, FAMILY,RELATIONS, FRIENDS & WORK	STABILIZES ALL TYPES OF COMMUNICATION IN ALL AREAS	STABILIZES ALL MATTERS OF THE HEART. PARENTS, KIDS, PETS, LOVERS	STABILIZES ALL MATTERS OF A PHYSICAL NATURE, SEX, HATE, LUST	I HARMONIZE / VENUS / INTROSPECTION

8 SCORPIO WATER Eight	TOO MUCH POWER & WEALTH, THE IRS INHERITANCE, LOSS A PARTNERS FUNDS	THE POWER OF THE MIND FOR TRANSFORMATION & MANIFESTATION	THE POWER THAT LOVE AND STRONG EMOTIONS CAN BRING	THE POWER OF BRUTE STRENGTH, SEX MAGICK, WAR, AND DEATH	I TRANSFORM MARS PLUTO POWER
9 SAGITTARIUS FIRE Nines	HUMANITARIAN MONITORY AID OR ADVICE GIVEN OUT OF CHARITY	HUMANITARIAN EDUCATION, LITERACY & THE SCIENCES	HUMANITARIAN THE HOMELESS, THE ABUSED, ALL VICTIMS	HUMANITARIAN ENVIRONMENT, WORLD AFFAIRS & NEEDY PEOPLE	I THEORIZE JUPITER HUMANITARIAN
10 CAPRICORN EARTH Tens	REBIRTH A MENTOR WITH MONEY AND POWER	REBIRTH COMPLETELY NEW WAY OF THINKING	REBIRTH TO REALIZE LOVE WHERE NO LOVE WAS BEFORE	REBIRTH REALIZATION FOR THE PROPER USE OF FORCE & FEAR	I REALIZE SATURN REBIRTH
11 AQUARIUS AIR Jacks/Princes/Pages & Princesses	MESSENGER NEWS OF MONEY GAIN, SUCCESS OR A WINDFALL	MESSENGER, TELEPATHY & CHANNELING INFORMATION	MESSENGER NEWS FROM OR ABOUT A LOVED ONE. MESSAGES OF LOVE	MESSENGER NEWS OF VICTORY, CONQUEST, WAR, VIOLENCE & ACTION	I DREAM SATURN URANUS MESSENGER
12 PICES WATER Knights/ Amazons	DRIVING FORCE TASK MASTER, WORK-A-HOLIC	DRIVING FORCE FOR KNOWLEDGE AND WISDOM	DRIVING FORCE TO FIND LOVE OR CONQUER A LOVE	DRIVING FORCE TO CONQUER, OWN, OR DESTROY	I CONTROL NEPTUNE JUPITER
Queens Hermaphrodite	I create, protect & reveal secrets of work/wealth	I create, protect & reveal secrets of wisdom	I create, protect & reveal secrets of love & pleasure	I create, protect & reveal secrets of movement/action	I create, protect & reveal secrets
Kings Hermaphrodite	I master opposition & give wise counsel / money	I master opposition & counsel wisdom	I master opposition & give wise counsel / love	I master opposition & give counsel on aggression / war	I master opposition & give wise counsel

Major Arcana / Part One

	ARIES — AM	TAURUS — ACQUIRE	GEMINI — COMMUNICATE	CANCER — PERCEIVE	LEO — EXPERIENCE	VIRGO — SERVE
FOOL INNOCENCE	ONE'S POTENTIAL	A FOOL AND HIS MONEY	HONESTY & SINCERITY	ROSE COLORED GLASSES	IRRESPONSIBILITY	NAIVE SERVICE TO OTHERS
MAGICIAN MANIFESTATION	DISCOVERY OF THE GOD/DESS WITHIN	MANIFESTING GREAT WEALTH	TO CREATE TROUGH COMMUNICATION	SENSITIVITY TO THE NEEDS OF FAMILY/AGED	MANIFESTING NEW KARMA IN THE PRESENT LIFE	TO GIVE OR DO FOR OTHERS
PRIESTESS KNOWLEDGE	DISCOVERY OF THE GOD/DESS WITHIN	A STUDENT / A SEEKER OF KNOWLEDGE	A TEACHER OF WISDOM AND KNOWLEDGE	DEVELOPING ONE'S PSYCHIC ABILITIES	USING THE KNOWLEDGE OBTAINED IN LIFE	GIVING WISE SERVICE TO OTHERS
EMPRESS ABUNDANCE	THE POTENTIAL TO CREATE ABUNDANCE	TO BECOME WEALTHY	A TEACHER OF WEALTH	TO SEE THE WEALTH IN FAMILY	WEALTH FROM THE CREATIVE ARTS, RISK, ETC.	PERSONAL SATISFACTION IN HELPING OTHERS
EMPEROR AMBITION	DRIVING FORCE A WORK-A-HOLIC	DRIVING & BLIND GREED	TO TEACH HOW TO GET AHEAD IN LIFE	DESIRE TO EMULATE ANOTHER	EXCELLING AT RISKS, GAMES AND CHALLENGE	CHURCHES, CHARITIES AND NON-PROFIT WORK
HIEROPHANT AUTHORITY	ANY PERSON IN OR OF POWER, POLICE / JUDGE	TO BECOME A PERSON OF MONEY / POWER	EXPRESSIVE POLITICIANS AND JUDGES	HEADS OF FAMILY AND HOUSEHOLD	ACHIEVERS IN SPORTS, GAMES, CRAFTSMEN	THE PERSON IN CHARGE / A BOSS OR SUPERVISOR
LOVERS UNION	LEARNING TO LOVE & ACCEPT ONESELF	TO PROFIT FROM PARTNERSHIPS, UNIONS	NEGOTIATOR & NEGOTIATIONS FOR OTHERS	WEDDINGS, ANNIVERSARIES & SPOUSES	SEXUAL UNION, BONDING WITH ANOTHER	JOINING GROUPS AND ORGANIZATIONS
CHARIOT CHALLENGE	DISCOVERING YOU ARE LIMITLESS	THE TASK OF ACQUIRING & KEEPING WEALTH	TOUGH SALES, ARBITRATIONS & NEGOTIATIONS	DIFFICULT RELATIONS WITH FAMILY / ELDERS	COMPETITIONS, & RISKS OF ALL TYPES	TRYING TO HELP THE UNGRATEFUL
STRENGTH COURAGE	BRAVERY AND STAMINA IN THE FACE OF ODDS	IN THE FACE OF LOSS OR GAIN, BEING HONEST	TO SPEAK THE TRUTH IN SPITE OF THE ODDS	TO STOP RELYING ON FAMILY FOR DECESIONS	BELIEVE & RELY ON YOURSELF IN COMPETITIONS	POLICE & FIRE FIGHTERS, RESCUE TEAMS
HERMIT INSPIRATION	EXPLORING THE REALMS OF THE INNERSELF	TO ENABLE & INSPIRE GREAT PHILOSOPHERS	MAGICK, OCCULT & SPIRITUAL TEACHERS	FAMILY CRISIS & GUIDANCE COUNSELORS	GENIUS IN ONE'S CHOSEN ACTIVITY	A CALLING TO HELP OTHERS

Card						
WHEEL OF FORTUNE / FATE	TO DISCOVER YOU CREATED YOUR DESTINY	THE RESPONSIBILITY WEALTH BRINGS	ORATOR OF LIFE & CONTROLLING ONE'S DESTINY	DISPOSITION OF FAMILY / LATER LIFE	WINNING OR LOOSING IN A CHOSEN FIELD	TO BE BORN THE SLAVE OR THE MASTER
JUSTICE / KARMIC LAW	WORKING WITH AND THROUGH KARMA	ACTION OR LACK OF, CREATES LOSSES / PROFITS	PHILOSOPHER, & TEACHER OF LIFE & KARMA	YOU'RE BORN INTO A FAMILY FOR LEARNING	EXPERIENCE ACCORDING TO PAST LIVES	WHAT YOU GIVE YOU RECEIVE NOW OR LATER
THE HANGED MAN / INDECISION	TO FEEL WEAK, HELPLESS & VULNERABLE	INVESTMENT QUANDARY HESITATION	TEACHING TO PAUSE & THINK BEFORE ACTING	UNCERTAINTY & HESITATION IN FAMILY MATTERS	CONFUSION & LACK OF ACTION DUE TO FEAR	CONCERN OVER SERVING SELF OR OTHERS FIRST
DEATH / TO TRANSMUTE	TO CHANGE PHYSICALLY	TO REBUILD DYEING PROFITS TO RECOVER	A PHILOSOPHER & TEACHER OF REINCARNATION	TO OBSERVE CHANGE IN ONE'S FAMILY	TO ALTER YOUR REALITY & EXPERIENCE	TO MAKE A DIFFERENCE BY YOUR EFFORTS
TEMPERANCE / BALANCE	TO BE IN HARMONY WITH YOURSELF	A BALANCE BETWEEN MONEY & HONESTY	TEACHING PEACE TO A VIOLENT WORLD	HARMONIOUS FAMILY RELATIONS	TO FOLLOW ONE'S INNER CALLING	TO BALANCE SERVICE WITH BEING SERVED
DEVIL / BONDAGE	A PERSON WHO MAKES OTHERS OWE THEM	A SLAVE TO GREED	A BOOK WORM PROFESSIONAL STUDENT	THE TIES OF FAMILY ARE AS CHAINS	ADDICTIONS OF ALL TYPES	A SLAVE OR SERVANT TO ANOTHER
TOWER / BIG CHANGES	ALTERATION IN OR ABOUT ONESELF	BANKRUPTCY & MONEY LOSSES	DOOMS DAY PREDICTORS & CHRISTIANITY	SWIFT CHANGES WITHIN THE FAMILY UNIT	REVERSALS IN ALL ASPECTS OF PRESENT LIFE	ALTERING A PRESENT SERVICE
STAR / HOPES, DREAMS and WISHES	THE DESIRES OF THINGS YET TO COME	THE GOAL OF OBTAINING WEALTH / POWER	TO DREAM OF FAME BY MEDIA COMMUNICATION	ASPIRATIONS OF HAVING ONE'S OWN FAMILY	TO ASPIRE GREATNESS IN A CHOSEN FIELD	DREAMS OF A SERVICE TO AID OTHERS
MOON / ILLUSIONS	AN IMPOSTER OR PHONY	A FALSE PRETENCE OF WEALTH	POOR INSTRUCTION & BAD ADVICE	THE APPEARANCE OF A FAMILY	DUPED BY CON ARTISTS	FAKE CHARITIES, INSTITUTES & CORPORATIONS
SUN / FULFILLMENT	DISCOVERING FULFILLMENT IS WITHIN	RAGS TO RICHES MONETARY HAPPINESS	HAPPINESS BY COMMUNICATING WITH OTHERS	THE FEELING OF COMPLETENESS A FAMILY BRINGS	IN ALL ASPECTS OF ROMANCE & CRAFTMANSHIP	FEELING THAT ONE HAS A REASON IN LIFE
JUDGMENT / REBIRTH	CHANGE CREATES A NEW OUTLOOK & YOU	RECOVERY FROM A BANKRUPTCY OR MONEY LOSS	A NEW UNDERSTANDING OR VIEW	TO SEE THROUGH THE EYES OF OTHERS	TO RADICALLY CHANGE ONE'S ENTIRE LIFE	THERAPISTS, COUNSELORS & PSYCHIATRISTS
THE WORLD / MASTERY & JOY	TO MASTER THE BODY AND INNERSELF	WEALTH & JOY THROUGH MONEY AND POWER	RENOWNED ORATORS	FATHER & MOTHERHOOD	FAMOUS ENTERTAINERS & CELEBRITIES	RESPECTED HUMANITARIANS

Major Arcana / Part Two

	LIBRA – Harmonize	SCORPIO – Transform	SAGITTARIUS – Theorize	CAPRICORN – Realize	AQUARIUS – Dream	PISCES – Control
FOOL INNOCENCE	CHILD-LIKE FORGIVENESS	AWAKENING TO THE INNER & OUTER WORLD	CONTEMPLATION OF SELF, REALITY & ONE'S WORLD	REALIZATION ALL IS NOT AS IT SEEMS	GOALS WITHOUT A REALISTIC FOUNDATION	THE CONTROLS OTHERS HAVE OVER YOU
MAGICIAN MANIFESTATION	PEACEFUL DIPLOMACY, A DIPLOMAT	RITUAL MAGICK SUMMONING THE SPIRITS	CREATING THE MAGICKAL GRIMORE	MASTER MAGICKAN / A WISE ONE	DREAM MAGICK AND THOUGHT FORMS	LEARNING TO CONTROL THE LIFE FORCES
PRIESTESS KNOWLEDGE	TEACHERS OF DIPLOMACY & LAW	THE SECRETS OF DEATH & IGNORANCE	THE ABILITY TO FATHOM THE UNFATHOMABLE	TO SEE BEYOND SPECULATION TO REAL KNOWLEDGE	THE SECRETS OF DREAMS REVEALED	LEARNING TO CONTROL THE UNCONTROLLABLE
EMPRESS ABUNDANCE	PROSPERITY THROUGH MEDIATION	TO CHANGE ABUNDANCE TO POVERTY	TO CALCULATE & MINIMIZE MONETARY RISK	GOALS ACHIEVED, SUCCESS	TO DREAM BUT NEVER HAVE SUCCESS	BANKERS, LANDLORDS, THE POWERFUL
EMPEROR AMBITION	TO BALANCE DRIVE WITH A CONSCIOUS	LAZINESS & COMPLACENCY	MOTIVATIONIST	TASK MASTER, A WORK-A-HOLIC	A SPINELESS & WEAK PERSON	A DICTATOR, SUPPRESSION OF $$$ FREEDOM
HIEROPHANT AUTHORITY	WATCH-DOG COMMITTEES AMBASSADORS	TO REVOLT OR RESTRAIN AUTHORITY	LAW MAKERS & GOVERNMENT BUREAUCRACY	A PROMOTION & EXERTING ONE'S POSITION/POWER	ASPIRATIONS FOR POWER & STRENGTH	REGULATORY BODIES, GOVERNORS
LOVERS UNION	JUSTICE OF THE PEACE & MARRIAGE	DIVORCE COURT & LAWYERS, TO SPLIT UP	MARRIAGE COUNSELORS & ARBITRATORS	SEXUAL UNION OR BONDING WITH ANOTHER	YOUTH, ROMANCE, WHITE KNIGHTS & DAMSELS	RELIGION, PARENTS, SOCIETY
CHARIOT CHALLENGE	TO NEUTRALIZE A CHALLENGE PREPARE FOR IT	TO CONQUER OBSTACLES & OBJECTIONS	THE CONTEMPLATION OF LIFE & PURPOSE	TO FACE OPPOSITION OR OBSTACLES	BOREDOM, TO DESIRE ADVENTURE	MANIPULATING ALL SITUATIONS
STRENGTH COURAGE	WISE ACTION LEADS TO SAFE HEROICS	A COWARD OR COWARDLY ACTION	BRAVADO OF THE ARM CHAIR KNOW-IT-ALL	THE UNEXPECTED HERO / HEROINE REAL HEROICS	STORY TELLERS, OLD-TIMERS SPINNING YARNS	MARTIAL LAW, TO REMOVE ALL HOPE
HERMIT INSPIRATION	BALANCING THE MATERIAL & SPIRITUAL SELF	CONFUSION, A BLOCKED CONDITION	TO CONTEMPLATE THE GOD/DESS AS PART OF SELF	TO MYSTERIOUSLY RECEIVE WISDOM OR INSPIRATION	GUIDANCE THROUGH DREAM MAGICK	VOLUNTARY CONTROL OF ALTERED STATES

Card						
WHEEL OF FORTUNE / FATE	OVERCOMING PERSONAL HANDICAPS	MANIPULATING FATE TO YOUR BEST ADVANTAGE	A PHILOSOPHY THAT YOU CONTROL FATE	FOR BETTER OR WORSE TO LIVE YOUR FATE	HOPES & DREAMS OF THINGS TO COME IN LIFE	THE MAGICKAN WHO CONTROLS HIS/HER FATE
JUSTICE / KARMIC LAW	TO UNDERSTAND KARMA & WORK THROUGH IT	LEARNING FROM PAST MISTAKES TO AVOID KARMA	A PHILOSOPHER OF COSMIC LAW AND ORDER	REAPING THE REWARDS OF PAST DEEDS	TO DREAM OF EVENTS IN PAST LIVES	MAGICKANS CONTROL THEIR KARMA
THE HANGED MAN / INDECISION	TO PHYSICALLY PAUSE OR HESITATE	TAKING SWIFT & IMMEDIATE ACTION	CONTEMPLATION OF ACTION VERSES INACTION	FROZEN, BLOCKED, UNABLE TO TAKE ACTION	UNABLE TO SEEK GUIDANCE THROUGH DREAMS	CALCULATING DECISIONS BASED ON LOGIC
DEATH / TO TRANSMUTE	TO COMPROMISE	ILLNESS, DEATH. ENDING	THE PHILOSOPHY, NOTHING DIES ONLY CHANGES	A PROFOUND EXPERIENCE THAT ALTERS ONE	USING DREAM MAGICK TO ALTER THE REAL WORLD	CONTROLING ENERGY TO CREATE CHANGE
TEMPERANCE / BALANCE	INDECISIVE, A FENCE WALKER, WISHY-WASHY	CHAOS	WIN WIN THINKING IS THE KEY TO HARMONY	INNER PEACE & HAPPINESS, LIKING ONESELF	TO DESIRE A PERFECT LIFE, MATE & WORLD	HARMONY BY MIND, DIET & BODY CONTROL
DEVIL / BONDAGE	MAKING A BAD SITUATION WORK FOR YOU	BREAKING FREE OF ALL THAT BINDS YOU	INSTITUTIONAL REFORMS & REFORMER	INCARCERATION, TAKING AWAY FREEDOM	LONGING FOR LOST FREEDOM	JAILER, WARDEN, BONDSMAN
TOWER / BIG CHANGES	PSYCHIATRISTS, COUNSELORS, & ARBITRATORS	CONFIDANTS, TO LESSON THE EFFECTS	TO STUDY CHOAS, AND REVOLUTION	UNEXPECTED EVENTS, TO REVOLT	CHANGING ONE'S GOALS & DESIRES IN LIFE	CONTROLLING REVOLTS & REVOLUTIONS
STAR / HOPES, DREAMS and WISHES	SEEKING GOALS THAT CREATE HAPPINESS	ENDING A DREAM TO MAKE ROOM FOR ANOTHER	THE STUDY OF DREAMS, RESEARCHERS	INSPIRATION OR GUIDANCE THROUGH DREAMS	LIVING IN & FOR THE WORLD OF DREAMS	MASTERY OF DREAM MAGICK & ASTRAL TRAVEL
MOON / ILLUSIONS	ACCEPTING THE FALSEHOODS OF OTHERS	MANIFESTING AN ILLUSION INTO A PHYSICAL REALITY	TO RESEARCH REALITY VERSES NON-REALITY	TO SEE PAST THE GUISE OTHERS WEAR	SEND A DREAM WITH A MESSAGE TO ANYONE	CONTROLLING WHAT OTHERS SEE BY MAGICK
SUN / FULFILLMENT	SATISFACTION WITH ONESELF & WORLD	UNHAPPINESS, DISCORD & DISSATISFACTION	TO HAVE IT ALL & BE UNHAPPY, TO STUDY WHY	SUCCESS IN ALL ENDEAVORS & IN ROMANCE	ASPIRATIONS FOR FUTURE HAPPINESS	MANIFESTING HAPPINESS BY MAGICK
JUDGMENT / REBIRTH	TO GIVE OR BE OFFERED A SECOND CHANCE	A NEAR DEATH EXPERIENCE, RECOVERY	THE PHILOSOPHY OF REINCARNATION	TO FEEL BORN ANEW FROM SOME EXPERIENCE	WALK-INS & TO AWAKE FEELING REBORN	OCCULT SECRETS OF BEING REBORN AT WILL
THE WORLD / MASTERY & JOY	THE FEELING OF STABILITY SUCCESS BRINGS	UNHAPPINESS & FAILURE, DISAPPOINTMENT	TEACHERS OF ACHIEVEMENT & WEALTH BUILDING	EXPERTISE & SUCCESS IN ALL ENDEAVORS	PLANNING WAYS TO ACHIEVE ONE'S GOALS	WITH MASTERY OF SELF COMES MASTERY OF JOY

THE HOUSES AND THEIR RELATED PROFESSIONS

NAME OF ZODIAC HOUSE	PROFESSIONS	
1 ♈ ARIES	SOLDIERS, FIRE FIGHTERS AND POLICE OFFICERS, MECHANICS, BODY BUILDERS, ATHLETES	MARS
2 ♉ TAURUS	FARMERS, RANCHERS, WINE GROWERS, LAND OWNERS, GROCERS, NURSERY OWNERS.	VENUS
3 ♊ GEMINI	ACCOUNTANTS, BANKERS, COMPUTER OPERATORS, LANGUAGE PROFESSORS, TEACHERS	MERCURY
4 ♋ CANCER	HOUSEWIVES AND HOUSEKEEPERS, JANITORS, CHEFS, BUTLERS, MAIDS, WINDOW WASHERS	MOON
5 ♌ LEO	ACTORS, ARTISTS, ARCHITECTS, BUILDERS, WELDERS, MUSICIANS.	SUN
6 ♍ VIRGO	NURSES, HOSPITAL AND FOOD SERVICE WORKERS, DOCTORS, SURGEONS, HEALERS, HERBALISTS, VETERANIANS-SMALL ANIMALS	MERCURY
7 ♎ LIBRA	COURT CLERKS, METER MAIDS, COURT STENOGRAPHER, JUDGES, LAWYERS, COUNSELORS	VENUS
8 ♏ SCORPIO	MORTICIANS, IRS AGENTS, ACCOUNTANTS, BOOK AND RECORD KEEPERS, GOVERNMENT AGENTS.	MARS PLUTO
9 ♐ SAGITTARIUS	ARCHEOLOGISTS, HISTORIANS, SCHOLARS, PROFESSORS, PHILOSOPHERS, RELIGIOUS LEADERS	JUPITER
10 ♑ CAPRICORN	LIVING LEGENDS, HERO'S AND HEROINES, WORLD LEADERS, ROYALTY, FAMOUS PERSONS, THE VERY RICH AND POWERFUL, POLITICIANS.	SATURN
11 ♒ AQUARIUS	SAILORS, SCUBA DIVERS, COMMUNITY WORKERS, THERAPISTS, MARINE BIOLOGISTS, UNION WORKERS	URANUS SATURN
12 ♓ PISCES	JAILERS, MATRONS, INSTITUTIONAL WORKERS, PAROLE OFFICERS, VETERANIANS - LARGE ANIMALS	NEPTUNE JUPITER

Zodiac Worksheet

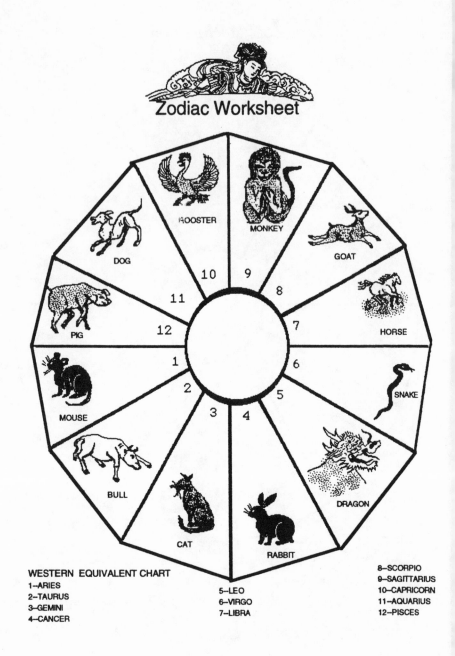

Zodiac Worksheet

WESTERN EQUIVALENT CHART

1—ARIES
2—TAURUS
3—GEMINI
4—CANCER

5—LEO
6—VIRGO
7—LIBRA

8—SCORPIO
9—SAGITTARIUS
10—CAPRICORN
11—AQUARIUS
12—PISCES

Appendix D

BIBLIOGRAPHY

(ISBN numbers and Publisher's addresses have been added to make obtaining the books easier.)

Amulets, Talismans, and Fetishes by Arthur S. Gregor, 1975. Published by Charles Scribner's Sons, New York, N.Y. ISBN 0-684-144603, Library of Congress Catalog Number: 74-26002

Ancient and Shining Ones, (The) by D. J. Conway. 1984. Self Published.

Practical Guide to The Runes, A, Their Uses in Divination and Magick by Lisa Peschel, 1989. Published by Llewellyn Publications, St. Paul, Minn. 55164-0383

Astrology, For the New Age by Marcus Allen, 1977. Published by Whatever Publishing, P.O. Box 3073, Berkeley, Calif. 94703. ISBN 0-931432-30-0.

Astrology, Wisdom of The Stars by Larry Kettlekamp, 1973. Published by William Morrow and Company, New York, N.Y. ISBN 0688-20085-0

Astrological Tarot, (The) by Georges Muchery, 1989. Published by Crescent Books and Distributed by Crown Publishers, Inc., 225 Park Avenue South, New York, N.Y. 10003. ISBN 0-517-68259-1

Book of Runes, (The) by Ralph Blum, 1982. Published by St. Martin's Press, 175 Fifth Avenue, New York, N.Y. 10010. ISBN 0-312-09002-1

Candle Magick Workbook (The) by Kala and Ketz Pajeon, 1992. A Citadel Press Book, Published by Carol Publishing Group, 600 Madison Avenue, New York, N.Y. 10022. ISBN 0-8065-1268-7

Choice Centered Tarot by Gail Fairfield, 1985. Published by Newcastle Publishing Co., Inc., North Hollywood, Calif. ISBN 0-87877-084-4

Complete Book of Amulets and Talisman (The), by Migene Gonzalez-Whippler, 1991. Published by Llewellyn Publications, A Division of Chester-Kent, Inc., P.O. Box 64383, St. Paul, Minn. 55164-0383. ISBN 0-87542-287-X

Complete Book of Spells, Ceremonies and Magick (The) by Migene Gonzalez-Whippler, 1991—Fifth Printing. Published by Llewellyn Publications, A Division of Chester-Kent, Inc., P.O. Box 64383, St. Paul, Minn. 55164-0383. ISBN 0-87542-286-1

Complete Book of the Occult and Fortune Telling, 1945. Published by Tudor Publishing Co., New York, N.Y.

Culpeper's Complete Herbal, by Nicholas Culpeper. Published by W. Foulsham & Co., LTD, New York, N.Y. ISBN 0-572-00203-3

Earth Mother Astrology, by Marcia Starck, 1989. Published by Llewellyn Publications, A Division of Chester-Kent, Inc., P.O. Box 64383, St. Paul, Minn. 55164-0383. ISBN 0-87542-741-3

Easy Tarot Guide, by Marcia Masino, 1987. Published by ACS Publications, Inc., P.O. Box 34487, San Diego, Calif. 92103-0802. ISBN 0-917086-59-7

Encyclopedia of Ancient and Forbidden Knowledge (The) by Zolar, 1970. Published by Fawcett Popular Library, CBS Educational and Professional Publishing, a division of CBS Inc. ISBN: 0-445-08449-0

Fortune Telling With Cards by P. Foli, 1969. Published by Melvin Powers Wilshire Book Company, 12015 Sherman Road No. Hollywood, Calif. 91605.

Fortune Telling by Tarot Cards, A Beginner's Guide to Understanding the Future Using Tarot Cards, by Sara Fenton, 1985. Published by Aquarian Press, Thorsons Publishing Group, Wellingborough, Northamptonshire, NN8 2RQ England. ISBN 0-85030-445-8

Fortune-Telling by Playing Cards, A New Guide to the Ancient Art of Cartomancy by Nerys Dee, 1982. Published by The Aquarian Press, Thorsons Publishing Group Wellingborough, Northamptonshire, NN8 2RQ, England. ISBN 0-85030-266-8

Fortune-Telling by Runes, by David and Julia Line, 1984. Published by The Auarian Press, Thorsons Publishing Group, Northamptonshire, NN8 2RQ, England. ISBN 0-85030-367-2

From One to Zero, A Universal History of Numbers, by Georges Ifrah, English Translation 1985. Published by Penguin Viking Inc., 40 West 23rd Street, New York, N.Y. 10010. ISBN 0-670-37395-8

Graphic Astrology, The Astrological Home Study Course, by Ellen McCaffrey, M.A., 1931, 1932, 1952. Published by Macoy Publishing Company, Richmond, Vir.

Galdrab (The), by Stephen E. Flowers, Ph.D., 1989. Published by Samuel Weiser, Inc. Box 612, York Beach, Maine. 03910. ISBN 0-87728-685-X

Healing Herbs of the Zodiac (The), by Ada Muir, 1986. Published by Llewellyn Publications, A Division of Chester-Kent, Inc., P.O. Box 64383, St. Paul, Minn. 55164-0383. ISBN 0-87542-486-4

Herbs, Health & Astrology, by Leon Petulengro, 1977. Published by Keats Publishing, Inc., by arrangement with Darton, Longman and Todd, Ltd., London, England. 0-87983-148-0

History of Astrology (The), by Zolar, 1972. Published by Arco Publishing Company, Inc., 219 Park Avenue South, New York, N.Y. 10003.

History and Practice of Magic (The), by Paul Christian, 1972, sixth printing. Published by Citadel Press, Inc., Publishers, 120 Enterprise Avenue, Secaucus, N.J. 07094. ISBN 0-8065-0126-X

History of Playing Cards, With Anecdotes of Their Use in Conjuring, Fortune-Telling and Card Sharping (The), edited by S. Taylor and others, 1973. Published by Charles E. Tuttle Company, Inc., of Rutland, Vermont, and Tokyo, Japan, Suido 1-chome, 2-6, Bunkyo-ku, Tokyo, Japan. ISBN 0-8048-1026-5. First Edition, 1865 by John Camden Hotten, London, England. First Tuttle edition, 1973, Second printing, 1983.

History of Western Astrology, A by Jim Tester, 1987. Published by St. Edmundsbury Press, Bury St, Edmunds, Suffolk, England. ISBN 0-85115-446-8

How to Tell Fortunes With Cards, Secrets of the Gypsies, by Wade Clayburn, 1988. Published by Globe Communications Corp., 441 Lexington Avenue, New York, N.Y. 10017

Introduction to the Study of the Tarot, by Oswald Wirth, 1983, Published by U.S. Games Systems, Inc., 38 East 32nd. Street, New York, N.Y. 10068. ISBN 0-88079-001-6, Library of Congress Catalog Card Number: 82-50753

Instant Astrology, by Mary Oser, Rich and Glory Brightfield, 1984. Published by ACS Publications, Inc., P.O. Box 16430, San Diego, Calif. 92116-0430. ISBN 0-917086-63-5

It's in the Cards, by Marthy Jones, 1980, in Dutch, reprinted 1986. Published by Samuel Weiser, Inc., Box 612, York Beach, Maine 03910. ISBN 0-87728-600-0

Karmic Tarot, by Wm. C. Lammey, 1988. Published by New Castle Publishing Co., Inc. ISBN 0-87877-136-0

Kwan Yin Book of Changes (The), by Diane Stein, 1985. Published by Llewellyn Publications, A division of Chester-Kent, Inc., P.O. Box 64383, St. Paul, Minn. 55164-0383. ISBN 0-87542-760-X

Leaves of Yggdrasil, by Freya Aswynn, 1990. Published by Llewellyn Publications, St. Paul, Minn. 55164-0383. ISBN 0-87542-024-9

Mandala Astrological Tarot (The), by A.T. Mann, 1987. Published by Harper and Row, Publishers, San Francisco, Calif. ISBN 0-06-250583-I

Manual of Occultism, A by Sepharial, 1979. Published by Newcastle Publishing Co., Inc. ISBN 0-87877-046-1

Medicine Wheel/Bear Tribe Publishing, 1978. P.O. Box 9167, Spokane, Wash. 99209 (a wheel, not a book)

Mirror of Magic (The), by Burt Seligmann, 1948. Published by Pantheon Books Inc., New York, N.Y.

Mystic Test Book, or the Magick of the Cards (The) by Olney H. Richmond, 1983. Published by New Castle Publishing Company, Inc., North Hollywood, California.

New Astrology (The), by Martin Seymour-Smith 1981. Published by Collier Books, Macmillan Publishing Co., 866 Third Avenue, New York, N.Y. 10022. ISBN 0-02-081940-4

New Feminist Tarot (The), by Jean Freer, 1987. Published by The Aquarian Press, Wellingborough, Northhamptonshire, England. ISBN 0-85030-563-2

Numbers and You, a Numerology Guide for Everyday Living, by Lloyd Strayhorn, 1987. Published by Ballantine Books, a division of Random House, Inc., New York, N.Y.

Numerology, Spiritual Light Vibrations, by Jeanne, 1987. Published by Your Center For Truth Press, P.O. Box 4094, Salem, Ore. 97302-8094. ISBN 0-9617877-0-8

Numerology, With Tantra, Ayurveda, and Astrology, by Harish Johari, 1990. Published by Destiny Books, One Park Street, Rochester, Vt. 05767. ISBN 0-89281-258-3.

Numerology Key to the Tarot, by Sandor Konraad, 1983. Published by Para Research, Inc., 85 Eastern Avenue, Gloucester, Mass. 01930. ISBN 0-914918-45-1, Library of Congress Card Catalog Number: 83-060062.

Numerology, Spiritual Light Vibrations, by Jeanne 1987 by Your Center For Truth Press, Published by Your Center of Truth Press, P.O. Box 4094, Salem, Ore. 97302-8094

Oracle of Geomancy, Techniques of Earth Divination (The) by Stephen Skinner, 1977. Published by Prism Press, Box 778, San Leandro, Calif. 94577, ISBN 0-907061-82-6

Origins of Astrology, by Jack Lindsay. Published by Barnes & Noble, Inc., New York, N.Y. 10003. ISBN 389-04118-1

Playing Card Workbook, A Contemporary Manual of Cartomancy (The), by Joanne Leslie, 1988. Published by The Aquarian Press, A Thorsons Company, Wellingborough, Northamtonshire, NN8 2RQ, England. ISBN 0-85030-743-0

Psychic Explorer (The), by Jonathan Cainer & Carl Rider, 1986. Published by Simon & Schuster Inc., A Fireside Book. Simon & Schuster Building, Rockefeller Center, 1230 Avenue of the Americas, New York, N.Y. 10020. ISBN 0-671-65945-6

Pocket I-Ching (The), by Gary G. Melyan & Wen-Kung Chu, 1977, third printing 1989. Published by Yenbooks, Charles E. Tuttle Company, Inc., Suido 1- Chome, 2-6 Bunkyo-ku, Tokyo, Japan. ISBN 0-8048-1566-6

Power Through Witchcraft, by Louise Huebner, 1971. Published by Bantam Books, Nash Publishing Corporation, 9255 Sunset Boulevard, Los Angeles, Calif. 90069.

Reading Your Future in the Cards, by Louise Woods, 1989. Published by Pocket Books, a division of Simon & Schuster Inc., 1230 Avenue of the Americas, New York, N.Y. 10020. ISBN 0-671-65821-2

Runelore, by Edred Thorsson, 1987. Published by Samuel Weiser, Inc., P.O. Box 612, York Beach, Maine 03910. ISBN 0-87728-667-1

Rune Magick, by Donald Tyson, 1988. Published by Llewellyn Publications, A Division of Chester-Kent, Inc., P.O. Box 64383, St. Paul, Minn. 55164-0383. ISBN 0-87542-826-6

Rune Might, by Edred Thorsson, 1989. Published by Llewellyn Publications, A Division of Chester-Kent, Inc., P.O. Box 64383, St. Paul, Minn. 55164-0383. ISBN 0-87542-778-2

Rune User's Handbook (The), by Tony Willis, 1987. Published by The Aquarian Press, A Thorsons Company, Wellingborough, Northamptonshire, NN8 2RQ, England.

Sacred Symbols of the Ancients, by Edith L. Randall and Florence Evylinn Campbell, M.A., 1989. Published by De Vorss & Company, Publisher, P.O. Box 550, Marina del Rey, Calif. 90294. ISBN 0-87516-487-0

Secret of the Runes (The), by Guido Von List and Edited, Introduced and Translated by Stephen E. Flowers, 1988. Published by Inner Traditions International, Ltd., One Park Street, Rochester, Vt. 05767. ISBN 0-89281-207-9

Solomon Manual of Divination and Ritual Spells (The), by Priscilla Schwei, 1988. Published by Llewellyn Publications, P.O. Box 64383, St. Paul, Minn., 55164-0383.

Spiritual, Astrological and Healing Values of Gems (The), by Willow, 1985. Published by Willow Jewelry, P.O. Box 8424, Emmeryville, Calif. 94662

Talking Drums to Written Word, How Early Man Learned to Communicate, by Gordon C. Baldwin, 1970. Published by Grosset & Dunlap, Inc., New York, N.Y. ISBN 0-448-21358-3, Library of Congress Card Number: 73-77851

Talismanic Magic, by Robin Skelton, 1985. Published by Samuel Weiser, Inc., Box 612, York Beach, Maine 03910. ISBN 0-87728-553-5

Tarot and Astrology, the Pursuit of Destiny, by Muriel Bruce Hasbrouck, 1986. Publisher Destiny Books, 377 Park Avenue South, New York, N.Y. 10016. ISBN 0-89281-121-8

Tarot Classic, by Stuart R. Kaplan, 1972. Published by U.S. Games Systems, Inc., New York, N.Y. 10016. ISBN 0-913866-55-5

Tarot for Your Self, by Mary Greer, 1984. Published by New Castle Publishing Co., Inc., North Hollywood, Calif. ISBN 0-87877-077-1. Tarot Constellations 1987, ISBN 0-87877-128-X. Tarot Mirrors, 1988, ISBN 0-87877-131-X.

Tarot Made Easy, by Nancy Garen, 1989. Published by Simon and Schuster, Simon and Schuster Building, Rockefeller Center, 1230 Avenue of the Americas, New York, N.Y. 10020. ISBN 0-671-67087-5

Tarot Spells, by Janina Renee, 1990. Published by Llewellyn Worldwide, LTD., P.O. Box 64383, St. Paul, Minn. 55164-0383. ISBN 0-87542-670-0.

Visual I Ching (The), by Oliver Perrottet, 1987. Published by Salem House Publishers, 462 Boston Street, Topsfield, Mass. 01983. An Eddison ● Sadd Edition, 2 Kendall Place, London W1H 3AH. ISBN 0-88162-265-6.

Wheel of Destiny, the Tarot Reveals Your Master Plan (The), by Patricia McLaine, 1991. Published by Llewellyn Publications, P.O. Box 64383, St. Paul, Minn. 55164-0383. ISBN 0-87542-490-2

Wheel of Fortune (The), by David and Julia Line, 1988. Published by Aquarian Press, Wellingborough, Northamptonshire, NN8 2RQ, England. ISBN 0-85030-618-3

Wild Witches Don't Get the Blues, Astrology Rituals & Healing, by Ffiona Morgan, 1991. Published by Daughters of the Moon Publishing, Box 357, Rio Nido, Calif. 95471

CHARTS AND GRAPHS

Elements of Astrology by Symbols and Signs, North Hollywood, California 91607.

CARDS

Tarot Tutor, An Instructive Book on Cards. Distributed by Tarot Tutor, Post Office Box 5974, Pasadena, California 91107.

ARTISTS' INFORMATION

Carol Law
% The Author
(All other Art)

Graphic Design
Created by Kala Pajeon using Computer Clip Art from:

Wet Paint Series Clip Art by Double Click
9316 Deering Avenue
Chattsworth, California 91311 U.S.A.
1-(800) 700-9525

Enzan-Hoshigumi Co., ***
Ste. 805, Harajuku Green Height
53-17, Sendagaya 3 Chrome
Shibuya-ku, Tokyo, 151 Japan

ABOUT THE AUTHORS

Kala and Ketz live in Northern California where they conduct research into various Metaphysical philosophies. Both are college graduates and combine their occult knowledge into their classes and writing of both fiction and non-fiction books.